PLUTO

THE POWER OF TRANSFORMATION

Maria Stiopei

Additional Inclusions by Alan Richards-Wheatcroft

Copyright © 2023 by Maria Stiopei

All Rights Reserved

Without limiting the rights reserved above under copyright, no part of this publication may be reproduced, stored in, or introduced into a retrieval system, or transmitted in any form or by any means (electronic, mechanical, photocopying, scanning, recording or otherwise), without written permission from both the author and the publisher, except in the case of brief quotations embodied in reviews and articles.

The scanning, uploading and distribution of this book via the Internet, or via any other means, without the written permission of the publisher is illegal and punishable by law. Please do not encourage electronic Cover

Requests and inquires may be mailed to:

American Federation of Astrologers (AFA)

6553 S. Rural Road

Tempe, AZ 85283, USA

ISBN: 978-0-86690-686-9

Cover design: Celeste Nash-Weninger

Images: Becris, shutterstock.com; 4des3, shutterstock.com

Published by: The American Federation of Astrologers (AFA), Tempe, AZ

www.astrologers.com

Acknowledgments

Thank You...

I want to thank Alan Richards-Wheatcroft for encouraging me to write this book. I would also like to thank him for keeping in touch with me during the entire process. Alan was my 'hidden teacher' throughout 2019. Previously, Alan had sent me all of his books, which I really enjoyed, and to which I would highly recommend to others. Over the years Alan has encouraged me to write, and I appreciate the fact that he believes in my potential. Furthermore, he trusts, and is inspired with my astrological knowledge. Alan opened up an opportunity, which supports one of my soul's wishes, which is to write a book. In other words, Alan gave me the opportunity to combine my knowledge with this project.

When I began to write, I immediately recognized my true vocational path, which according to my life force energy is to serve humanity. I simply love practising astrology, and people. Furthermore, I love writing about both of these topics allows me to fulfil the purpose of the soul in physical incarnation.

Additionally, Alan discovered the intercepted Pluto in my natal chart; this is an astrological concept that was unfamiliar to me, but it pressed me to find out more information about the meaning of interceptions. I always wanted to write books, but I never thought this journey would begin with Pluto. Being able to write this book has presented me with an opportunity to be able to interpret the natal chart through an entirely new perspective.

Once again, I would like to thank Alan for this mutual collaboration. Without your support, my thoughts and ideas may not have been brought into consciousness; therefore, this book would not have been compiled. I hope this shared collaboration will just be the beginning of something that could be beneficial to others. I will always be grateful and honored to be given this opportunity.

Also, I would like to thank Dave Campbell. He is the author of *Solving Crime with Astrology* — a very well-written book. Dave's work inspired me, especially when I began to link traditional astrology with this specific area of forensic research. I always knew that astrology could be beneficial to criminology.

At that time, I didn't discover many books on the subject; therefore, I have developed my own theory — through research. However, when I discovered Dave's book, I found that somebody else had explored this subject in a greater capacity. Moreover, his book included the asteroids, which interested me further. Thus, after reading his book, I was further motivated to expand my research — through other individuals and organizations. Now, I understand Dave's work.

I would also like to thank Marcela Andaluz for allowing me to be involved with her during such an important astrological event. It was during this that I made the connection to other astrologers, especially from all over the world. For me, it was a privilege to welcome them, and to watch them work — beautiful and humble souls. I was in awe of the astrological vibes; and I felt the energy of so many spiritual souls and teachers to whom I respect.

I would now like to thank one of my respected teachers from the Faculty of Astrological Studies, Gloria Roca. Gloria has greatly assisted me during the past few years with my studies; and she has enhanced my astrological viewpoint, especially with the way I now comprehend astrology. Gloria helped me to further understand aspects — inspiring me to look more deeply into the meaning of each aspect. Gloria has been very supportive and clear in her teachings.

Lastly, I would like to say Thank You to the American Federation of Astrologers, for publishing my work in your amazing monthly journal, and for sending me the Journal of Research. I have discovered the AFA to be a very well-organized organization, which has many members, thus offering the possibility to learn astrology in different ways. I value my membership, and for this reason, I would highly recommend the AFA to anyone like-minded, or to those who wish to expand upon their knowledge.

Table of Contents

Acknowledgements   iii

Section One
  Additional Inclusions by Alan Richards-Wheatcroft:
  Introduction   ix
  The Psychology of Evolution   xvii

Section Two
  Pluto and the Power of Transformation by Maria Stiopei:
  Chapter One:
  Pluto in the Trajectory of Human History   1
  Chapter Two:
  Pluto in Complicity with other Planets   13
  Chapter Three:
  Pluto Transits the Natal Chart   75
  Chapter Four:
  Pluto transiting the Charts of Other Countries   91
  Chapter Five:
  Pluto in a Powerful Organization's Chart   107
  Chapter Six
  Saturn-Pluto Conjunction- with Jupiter Transiting   115

Section Three
  Additional Pluto Inspections by Maria Stiopei:
  The Transformation of Romania   119
  Pluto and China   125

Section Four
  Chart Data:
  Equal House Systems   129

Introduction

"Pluto represents the power to transform. It first destroys; then rebuilds and regenerates. It rules death, destruction, obsession, subversion, crime, the underworld and that which is hidden. It governs phobias, bacteria, viruses and waste. Pluto represents stark reality, the naked truth, and the loss of innocence. It forces us to look inward and confront our darkest fears. When we face our demons, our lives are transformed and enriched."

Insightful Psychics

Pluto and Transformation

Simply speaking, transformation means to *surpass* hate with love. This is the principal meaning that is attached to the Venus-Pluto polarity. Transformation is the essential theme of this book.

Maria's book represents a compendium of information, which is extensive. This is because it characterizes many 'iconic figures,' and current 'state leaders,' and who have pronounced positions of Pluto in the natal chart. In addition, the book examines a carefully chosen selection of prominent figureheads, who have each been responsible for orchestrating discernible transformational *shifts* in power throughout the course of our historical and contemporary evolution. Insurgent, technological, and stimulating transferences of energy have been both calamitous and liberating within the global world order.

Moreover, some of these powerful Pluto character influences have brought us to our current state of technological and seemingly cataclysmic evolution, which is becoming more evident, especially now that Pluto is about to enter subversive and revolutionary Aquarius in 2023. Currently, we are all faced with critical decisions — direct from the center of the Pluto archetype.

Do we face ultimate destruction, hence the annihilation and elimination of the species? Or do we move towards the generational rebirth of the species? Hence, to embrace ultimate Pluto transformation by eliminating the principles of darkness — concerned primarily with obsessive behaviour, immorality and powerplay. These negative Pluto characteristics have always been evident; however, they have been *personified* recently by the likes of Kim Jong Un and Vladimir Putin.[1] Both of these so-called leaders feature as two of Maria's persuasive case studies.

No matter how difficult and devastating life can be, Pluto implies that we possess the power to 'rise up,' and move out of the smouldering ashes of our limitations, and our shortcomings. Furthermore, Pluto provides us with the power to embrace a new way of life –wholly new creations which are *reinforced* by the light. This powerful impression symbolizes the remarkable power of Pluto transformation, and its mythical symbol, the Phoenix.[2] Currently, the world is in urgent need of positive transformation – individually and collectively – before humankind faces the prospect of total and permanent annihilation and the elimination of the species.

A large percentage of Maria's case studies, however, have tried to assist with the transformation of individuals, through personally motivated assignments, and innovations. Ultimately, individual transformation invariably *inspires* the collective supremacy of humankind because they have been created out of love. These case studies include Steven Spielberg, Bill Gates, Joyce Carol Oates, and Thomas Hardy – each hoping that they will bring about a *recognition* of the truth – and a *need* to *inspire* and *transform* the individual with their notable proclamations.

Inspiration is a characteristic that orchestrates physical and psychological change; hence inspiration *inflames* the power of Pluto transformation. A diagram of Pluto's power of transformation is outlined below.

Pluto and Annihilation

Annihilation is a powerful Pluto indicator – epitomizing the point of expiration. Thus, annihilation will always be *masterminded* by individuals who become obsessed with the power to manipulate. Manipulation is also a Pluto characteristic. Thus, manipulation has always been used as a principal measure throughout the course of our current evolution. In addition, the ability to manipulate seems to be a key factor within the Pluto in Leo and the Pluto in Scorpio generations.

Perhaps, the power of Pluto is simply too overwhelming for many of these generational souls to endure? It certainly seems to be the case with Kim Jong Un (Pluto in Scorpio), and Vladimir Putin (Pluto in Leo), who have not only annihilated and condemned their own souls but have annihilated so many within the collective, souls who were just unfortunate to become victims of their power manipulation. However, these two soul groups have the greatest potential towards soul transformation. This is because Pluto is domicile in its ruling sign of Scorpio, and Pluto has the potential to *shine* like the Sun, which rules Leo (for more information refer to the following inclusion: The Psychology of Evolution).

Pluto's power is twofold; hence death (expiration and Scorpio) and rebirth (transformation, powered by the Sun). However, if annihilation occurs on a planetary scale, transformation will *not* be possible. This is because it would symbolize the 'end of evolution.' Therefore, transformation is a slow-moving process that is administered within the course of a single evolution; and which is signified by Pluto's tenure of the twelve signs of the zodiac (refer to The Psychology of Evolution).

Throughout the course of our evolution, some of history's iconic figures have brought the prospect of global annihilation nearer. This notion is comparable to our current dilemma, because some of the current world leaders are, through unawareness, *managing* the prospect of annihilation – by underscoring the probability of global elimination.

Illness and disease are also 'destructive Pluto indicators' – symbolizing the potential for the annihilation and elimination of the species. Humankind has recently witnessed the element of elimination due to the birth of the Covid-19 pandemic, which was initially powered by Pluto and its conjunction with Jupiter and Saturn in 2020 (for more information refer to Chapter Five).

Pluto's Biological Complexities

Principally, the proliferation of illness and disease symbolizes a distinct lack of Pluto-orientated transformation in the world. Essentially, transformation is a remote concept that is very much in *decline*. Primarily, this is because of a lack of creativity, caused, in part, by the negative conditioning of world leaders, operating via manipulation, as opposed to love. As a result, humankind continues to be *tyrannized* by a multitude of infirmities and disabilities, which are connected, in so many cases, with the Pluto physical hallmark, the colon.

Meanwhile, Pluto represents a 'powerful nucleus,' of enormous influence. The colon is, in effect, the essential nucleus of Pluto, which also needs to evolve via its principal element of transformation. Colon evolvement occurs via spiritual stillness and improved physical nutrition. That way, the colon produces less waste – lessening the likelihood of toxic contamination within the body. Today, there is so much waste and superfluous emptiness in the world – personifying our anticipation for illness and disease – spearheading the prospect of annihilation.

Ironically, many of the figureheads that Maria examines have, at some point, contracted a Pluto-related condition – originating in most cases from the colon. For example, Charles de Gaulle (one of Maria's case studies), the French army officer and statesman who led France against the oppression of Nazi Germany in World War II, developed prostate cancer.[3] The prostate is an organ denoting the potential for Pluto transformation. This is because its primary purpose is to produce the fluid that nourishes and transports sperm. Initially, prostate cancer is caused by a build of solid waste in the colon, which is transformed into liquid waste, which is highly toxic.[4] Thus, annihilation in the form of biological disease occurs within the physical body.

Ironically, because there was so much annihilation and elimination surrounding de Gaulle, which was caused by the war, he became entrenched *solely* within the Pluto vibration of death. Interestingly, in his natal chart, de Gaulle has Pluto domiciled in the eighth house of death and the colon, which opposes his Scorpio Sun, which is anaretic, at twenty-nine degrees (see chart 8). Anaretic degrees are, until transformed, representative of death. Although the eighth house is essentially a public domain, de Gaulle was so *enmeshed* by transforming the lives of others, he most likely neglected to transform his own Pluto nucleus, hence his soul.

In the present, it has been widely reported by the military media, that Vladimir Putin (another one of Maria's case studies) has contracted bowel cancer. Some have even suggested that his condition was the *catalyst* for the invasion of Ukraine. If Vladimir Putin has indeed contracted bowel cancer, it is most likely because of a lack of transformation (love) in his life. A lack of love was always evident in his life; primarily because Putin always appeared *unfriendly* and *expressionless*.

Speaking in a psychological capacity however, Vladimir Putin *lives* in the past. Thus, Putin wants Russia back to the way it was – operating as a combined communist state regime, similar to when it was the USSR. In Putin's natal chart, Pluto squares Jupiter (see chart 32). Thus, Putin finds it difficult to move onwards and upwards, especially in a psychological capacity. Therefore, he *stubbornly* places Pluto obstacles on his Jupiter journey for social distinction. But the days of communist rule have long passed, and Putin must transform his spirit into the here and now, if he is going to survive his Earth transition. Furthermore, Putin must accept the 'changing of the world,' as displayed by

Pluto's close conjunction to the MC in his natal chart.

Figureheads like Vladimir Putin, and so many more, are examined *meticulously* by the author Maria Stiopei. Maria's evolutionary knowledge and insight is nothing short of *exemplary*. This book characterizes an evolutionary journey through the chronicles of Pluto's evolutionary history.

Pluto's Nucleus — the Center of Transformation

'Pluto affirms that new thoughts and new age terminology refer primarily to the practice of positive thinking and self-empowerment fostering a belief that a positive mental attitude will achieve success in creative endeavours.'

Written by an unknown source, this, in my opinion, pertains towards the symbolic meaning of *transformation*, which is Pluto's primary characteristic.

Surely, Pluto's essential hallmark for creative, evolutionary and spiritual transformation begins at its central nucleus, as it does with every planet. Astrology operates on the premise that energy is transformed at the center of each planet in the cosmos via planetary interaction – its geometric aspects.

Pluto's Upholding of Degenerate Waste

Pluto's nucleus is considered to be the most powerful of all the planets. Indeed, the colon, which is Pluto's physical organ, is more or less situated at the center of the human body – the point in which every illness and disease begins. In addition, the colon is connected to the rectum, and the anus – extremities in which physical and psychological waste passes through – psychological waste is essentially flatulence. The movement of waste through these organs is sometimes referred to as the 'rear end' of transformation.[5] Containment of waste products, such as constipation, occurs when there is a distinct lack of creative transformation in life, and which ultimately depletes Pluto's power in the natal chart.

The reason why so many of the world's leaders have *failed* to instigate positive transformation in the world is because they are essentially operating from their rear ends so to speak, upholding degenerative waste. This is why they succumb to colon-related diseases. This is certainly the case where Vladimir Putin and Kim Jong Un are concerned. In essence, what they initiated is 'mere waste,' which, in this case, is driven by Pluto's depleted and contaminated power.

Pluto and Redevelopment

Unfortunately, very few souls operate from the heart center, hence from the nucleus of the physical body. When we chose to operate from the nucleus, evolutionary and creative transformation occurs *naturally*. Moreover, the colon remains a protected organ, and the waste that passes through it is purer. Therefore, there would be no colon-related illness and disease present in life.

Furthermore, transformation in its many guises would transition via each Pluto soul generation, which is indicative to Pluto's tenure of each sign of the zodiac, and Venus at Pluto's polarity (refer to The Psychology of Evolution). Thus, when individuals yield to the power of love, rather than to hate and manipulation, they become one of the most powerful individuals upon the Earth. Principally, this is Pluto's central standpoint. Thus, it is the ultimate power of transformation – released from its central (heart) nucleus.

If then, Pluto represents the most distant but *distinct* nucleus of the cosmos —recognizing its sole purpose of psychological and evolutionary transformation, surely this planet would be one of the most important and powerful spheres in the cosmos? The sole purpose of every planetary nucleus is to assist in the transformational process of Pluto's programme of redevelopment in the natal chart. Appropriately then, this intricate but intense procedure represents the authentic meaning of evolutionary transformation.

The primary purpose of every state leader is to orchestrate evolutionary transformation for the collective of the country they rule over.

Pluto's Innermost Nucleus, which Denotes the Power of Transformation

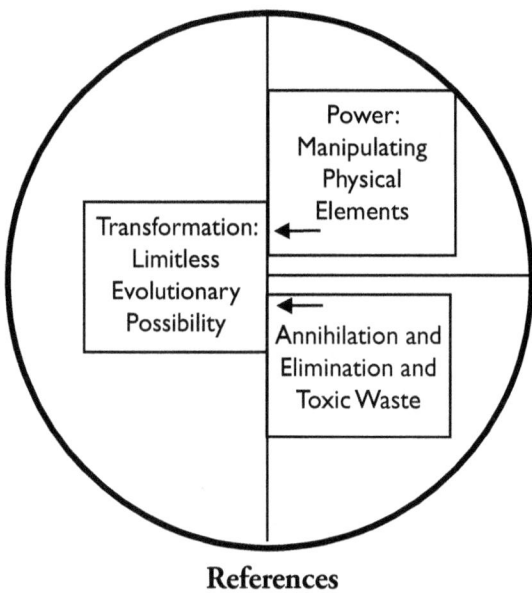

References

[1] Kim Jong UN is the president of North Korea. Vladimir Putin is the president of Russia.
[2] www.mythus.fandom.com.
[3] Information source *Wikipedia*.
[4] Information source *Wikipedia*.
[5] Information source www.fascrs.org.

The Psychology of Evolution

"It is not the strongest of the species that survives, nor is it the most intelligent that survives. It is the one that is the most adaptable to change, that lives within the means available, and works co-operatively against common threats."

Charles Darwin

Throughout the natural course of evolution, individuals have generally preferred the power of *preservation*, rather than the power of *transformation*. Principally, preservation means to hold on, especially to that which is *familiar* in some way. This is why illness and disease have always been common factors upon the Earth. In almost all cases, illness and disease are conditions that are set in motion when the soul *refuses* to acknowledge its birth right, which is to progress in a psychological and spiritual capacity, while incarnate. According to the *Akashic Records*, this is the elemental construct for spiritual evolution.

Darwinism, however, is the theory of biological evolution developed by the English naturalist, Charles Darwin. Darwin had a very pronounced position of Pluto in his chart, residing in the visionary sign of Pisces. It was also conjunct a domicile Mercury, and Jupiter in the third house of communication, and squared the Ascendant (see chart). Despite impending criticism of his life's work, Darwin was nevertheless able to communicate his conjectures in an impulsive, ardent, and confident manner. Thus, he eventually convinced the establishment that his theory of evolution, was in fact an image of real-life events.

Pluto, the planet most associated with the natural course of evolution, is often feared, because its psychological element of evolutionary transformation means to *progress* into unfamiliar territory. Evolutionary Transformation therefore requires courage, and strength of spirit – necessary characteristics for the wellbeing of the individual, and the collective.

Undoubtably, Pluto is a complexly transformational planet. Thus, the power of evolutionary transformation is an extensive conception; and one which is *facilitated* and *developed* through Pluto's psychology of evolution – Pluto's passage through the twelve signs of the zodiac. Furthermore, Pluto's power of transformation represents a psychological image of the future — something salutary to aim for — like the Phoenix that emerged from the ashes of its earlier existence. The Phoenix is an evolutionary representation of Pluto, and its ruling sign, Scorpio.

Karmically speaking, Pluto's power of transformation represents a crucial staging post – residing on the measured wheel of evolution. Essentially, these staging posts are symptomatic to the reincarnation of the soul, and its capacity for physical and spiritual development.

Evolutionary Inherencies

For the most part, a human being incarnates with an ingrained image of an inherent affliction. Exactly how an affliction manifests physically is entirely dependent on our subjective desire for transformation. If our desire is merely for preservation, then at some point on our evolutionary journey, the affliction will manifest – substantiated by Pluto's celestial sign. Therefore, the imposing complexity of the inherent affliction is *reflected* through Pluto's ruling sign.

So, for example, if Pluto tenants the sign of Leo, the inherent affliction will most likely be connected to the physical heart. Thus, it may be that a relative died from a heart condition. However, if we examine the evolutionary journey of the relative who died from the heart condition, it may well reveal that little or no soul transformation was actually obtained during their life. It may also reveal that the individual endured the heart condition for many years.

Physical transformation is possible via the other planets and points in the natal chart. However, 'psychological (unsurpassed) transformation' is only achieved through the Pluto archetype, and via its primary cosmic influence, the celestial sign that Pluto tenants in the natal chart. Therefore, unsurpassed transformation accounts for psychological and evolutionary (soul) transformation.

Pluto Iniquity

All throughout history, Pluto's power has been continually *corrupted*. As a result, mankind has *furnished* his evolutionary timeframes with mostly rapacious tendencies. Just how extreme the psychological boundaries within these immoral timeframes were was dependent solely on the disposition of Pluto's celestial sign. Perhaps, one of the most notorious of all the generational time frames, and which was considered mostly as a dark realm, was the Victorian period. Thus, the Victorian period was very much powered by Pluto, at its most *obstructive* and *fatalistic* of influences.

The Victorian period (1837-1901) was symbolized as a dark phase in our collective evolution. Principally, this is because it housed severe eye-watering crimes, such as violent theft, violent affray, child prostitution, and calculated murder – shadowed by intense darkness. Throughout the Victorian era, Pluto tenanted the signs of Aries (ruled by Mars), Taurus (ruled by Venus) and Gemini (ruled by Mercury). These types of crimes would also coincide with the ruling planetary influences of these signs – operating at the lowest vibration of influence. At the same time, the Victorian period was a low vibrational influence, captured within the historical chronicles of darkness. In effect, Pluto operating from these signs, accompanied by the dominating influences of the Victorian period, created a confluence of darkness and evil – corrupting Pluto's power.

Evolutionary Transformation

Meanwhile, it is important to emphasize, that it is very *unlikely* that individuals who were born into the Pluto in Aries, Taurus and Gemini generations, prior to the Pluto in Cancer generation of 1914, are still alive today. Therefore, it would be difficult to complete an analysis with regards to Pluto in these signs, particularly at that time. Nor, is it possible to theorize and predict the future outlook and conditions that will be associated with these same generational soul groups – proceeding the Pluto in Pisces generation, which culminates in 2067. Thus, we can only speculate as to the effects of these futuristic sojourns of Pluto.

During these early periods in history, there were of course remarkable individuals, who strived towards unsurpassed transformation. For example, from the Pluto in Gemini generation, came someone who transformed the lives of so many during the second World War, Nicholas Winton. Winton was born just before the advent of Pluto's transit of Cancer. His greatest achievement was to supervise the rescue of 669 children, most of them Jewish, from Czechoslovakia, on the eve of the second world war – an operation that was later referred to as the Czech *Kindertransport*. He also found homes for them and arranged for their safe passage to Britain.[1]

In this natural chart (birthtime unknown), Pluto's mythical brother Neptune tenants the sign of nurturing Cancer and opposes Uranus. In this case, the opposition means to liberate (Uranus/Neptune) the children (Cancer), under duress caused by the opposition. Pluto of course was in Gemini, and trines determined Mars in the humanitarian sign of Aquarius – recapitulating the emphasis of the Uranus-Neptune opposition. Gemini is naturally ruled by Mercury (communication), and Pluto is transformation. Winton successfully communicated his intent (Mercury) to the British authorities, in order to establish a new life (Pluto), for these children. Mercury is also conjunct Pluto in the chart. Thus, Winton possessed great power, which he used to influence the masses.

In my opinion, this was a truly remarkable accomplishment, which denotes psychological and evolutionary transformation. Nicholas Winton will no doubt be remembered in the Pluto archives, which records great achievements – symbolizing individual and collective transformation.

The Evolution of the Dark Night

The evolution of the dark night is a metaphor for a prolonged period of intense cruelty. Therefore, the Pluto-Aries-Taurus-Gemini generations that influenced all of civilization prior to 1914, are considered by many evolutionists to be the epochs which marked the beginning of 'the evolution of the dark night.' Perhaps then, the evolution of the dark night symbolized the ultimate preservation of evolution? Characteristically, the evolution of the dark night symbolized the beginning of the Victorian period, which was also a manipulative, warlike, and sexually-orientated epoch – packed full of Pluto duplexities and ambivalences.

Meantime, if memory serves, the evolutionary astrologer Jeffrey Wolf Green, remarked on something similar in one of his lectures, which took place in Cleveland, Ohio, in 2014. He remarked on the darkness surrounding this particular Pluto era. In every aspect of Victorian society, soul transformation was a far cry from the truth. This was Pluto plying its power at its lowest quality. In many ways, we are all still experiencing the negative impacts associated with this pitiless, obsessive and compulsive time span, especially where the nature of crime is concerned. Today, crimes have become more intense. This is particularly the case in the UK, and in other parts of the Pluto-influenced societies of the world.

Furthermore, for those souls who consider themselves as being creative geniuses, inspired visionaries, and the intellectuals of transformation, the evolution of the dark night must have seemed as being a calamitous and environmentally unfriendly blip, cast upon the wheel of evolution. These propensities are particularly relevant to the individuals who are part of the Pluto in Leo-Virgo and Scorpio soul groups.

Ideally, the evolution of the dark night should have represented a time when inspirational idealism, innovation and creativity should have taken precedent. Therefore, the evolution of the dark night should have been remembered as the beginning of the 'age of enlightenment.'[2] Instead, the evolution of the dark night was transformed into a source of corrupted power, especially towards the onset of World War I. Unfortunately, the individuals who lost their lives during the conflict of wars were mostly denied the opportunity for evolutionary transformation.

The oscillating backwash emanating from this destructive era is only now beginning to *dissipate*. During these latter stages of this dark epoch, the prospect of environmental and social catastrophes, and financial meltdowns, coupled with medically induced tragedies are likely to be severe. Strange as it may seem, these afflictions are necessary for global transformation. For example, the recent Covid-19 pandemic symbolized the beginning of an essential period of Pluto (purging) transformation – setting apart the start of widespread unification – within the cooperative and corporate powers of the world. The Covid-19 pandemic took hold during Pluto's final passage through Capricorn. Therefore, during Pluto's late transit of Capricorn, we may begin to witness a raft of other violent disturbances, all vying for power and control.

Meanwhile, Pluto's lengthy tenure of Capricorn has generated a transformational turning point – directing us slowly *away* from the long dark night.

Unsurpassed Evolutionary Transformation

Whatever Pluto soul group each of us belong to, it is not too late to *transform* the very essence of the dark night, before we all enter into the concluding chapter – namely the ultimate endgame for humankind which takes effect from 2067. However, from 2024, Pluto begins its humanitarian, philanthropic and consolidating passage through Aquarius, so we, as a collective, can begin to *heal.*

From its Capricorn station however, Pluto has *decimated* the financial economies of so many countries worldwide. However, had greed not been such a prolific influence, Pluto in Capricorn would have *transformed* the corporate economies of the into something more substantially favourable for all concerned. Furthermore, Pluto's transit of Capricorn would have provided liveable wages for all the working citizens of the world. For the retired there would be beneficial state pensions — increasing in value every year — in line with other costs and inflation. In addition, there would be free health care for all. These are all fundamental transformations associated with the Pluto archetype. Unfortunately, many countries have currently *capped* increases in pensions, all because of the influence of corporate greed and the Covid pandemic.

Meanwhile, if this current predicament of greed prheservation continues and reaches Pluto's entry into Aries in 2067, humankind will be faced with global catastrophe. At this point, the Earth will no longer support the infrastructure of humankind, hence a continuation of progression upon the evolutionary wheel of development. This information is recorded in the *Akashic Records* (see Footnote)

In order to avoid the prospect of a Pluto cataclysm, we need to begin embracing our spiritual roots. This is achieved by remembering who we really are at the source, hence the heart seed. Embracing our spiritual roots is achieved through stillness and contemplation, hence meditation. Advocating the use of meditation is perhaps the ultimate Pluto soul transformation. The illusion associated with time acceleration occurs because human beings are no longer still.³

Furthermore, we really need to start *repairing* the Earth by *enveloping* it with love and light, through heartfelt visualization, and group meditations. These are Pluto collective soul transformations. Alternatively, if we chose to continue on our current path, complete with all of our catastrophic propensities, a Pluto-type cataclysm, such as simultaneous volcanic eruptions is inevitable.

Footnote: *According to Wikipedia, the Akashic Records are a compendium of all universal events, thought, words, emotions and intent, which has occurred in the past, present or future, in terms of all life forms and entities, not just human.*

I would now like to examine the twelve signs of the zodiac and their innovatory effects upon the Pluto archetype. Each celestial sign represents a 'baseline characteristic' of Pluto's preservative, transformational and psychological power — powering the natal chart. Furthermore, if we were to look through a cosmic lens, one that contains the image of Pluto, we would be able to view the natal chart as a psychological conduit, which masterminds the capability for evolutionary (soul) transformation.

Individually, we can distribute the potential for transformation to the other members of our Pluto soul group — for the purpose of evolutionary propagation. According to the *Akashic Records*, the Neptune and Pluto soul groups *reflect* the soul groups we belong to in spirit. Furthermore, the celestial signs that both Neptune and Pluto tenant symbolize the strength (Neptune's sign) and the purpose (Pluto's sign) of the soul, while incarnate.

Yet, how this power is perceived and distributed throughout the natal chart is determined by the natal aspects to Pluto, and by Pluto transits to the natal planets. The celestial signs merely act as cosmic filters — discharging power accordingly.

From each sign however, Pluto functions primarily as a generational influence, as we shall now discover.

The Pluto in Cancer Generation: 1914 – 1939 (Approximate Dates)

For this particular soul group, the seeds of inherent illness and disease were most likely sown throughout childhood – only to be *extended* and *exhibited* throughout later life. Furthermore, the potential for illness and disease is strongly indicated when there are hard aspects from Pluto to other planets in the natal chart, particularly to the Moon and Saturn.

The way in which an infirmity sprouts, grows and develops, so to speak, is solely dependent on the method by which the individual choses to traverse the natural course of their evolutionary pathway. If the individual wanders through life *blindly*, then the onset of illness and disease is assured. This notion is of course relevant to all of the soul groups. However, for this group, the presence of inherent anxiety, especially in early life, has no doubt left its mark, in the form of a psychological blemish – imprinted on their otherwise sensitive personalities. Throughout life this psychological scar has slowly become discoloured – leading to the outbreak of illness and disease. It has also left them feeling defensive and insecure.

Furthermore, it is almost certain that this defensive and mostly insecure generation experienced an intensely difficult childhood. The Pluto in Cancer soul group require unending amounts of love and reassurance, above and beyond the other evolutionary groups. However, their parents would have found it difficult to honor these commitments, probably because they, too, were busy negotiating ways to *survive* the conflict of war.

Individually, those from the Pluto in Cancer group may have experienced the loss of a parent in early life, particularly to the ravages of war. But whatever the reasoning behind their inherent anxiety, this group continues to shoulder a great psychological weight – almost as if it is a natural part of their inherent programming. The Pluto in Cancer generation have become *united* in their grief. Thus, they have become united with each other. Figuratively speaking, they invented the term 'unified collective.'

Moreover, the Pluto in Cancer soul group have an inbuilt inclination towards the preservation of innocence, recollection and sentimentality. Therefore, this particular soul group are the masters of revisiting the past. Psychologically speaking, they frequently revisit the past to try to reason with it. This is a potentially dangerous endeavour; and that is why they have become particularly prone to dementia — surpassing all of the other Pluto soul groups.

The Pluto in Cancer generation represent a watertight embodiment of souls. Thus, they have traversed the path of life in a manner that can only be described as circumspect and discreet – assembling security and stability as their principal objectives. Nothing will deter them from their aims and their aspirations, which are mostly to build a better future, especially for their loved ones.

If they can naturally eliminate insecurity from their lives, the Pluto in Cancer generation will fundamentally become a less defensive soul group. Most of the time this in-depth generation likes nothing more than to nurture, and care for their fellow human beings – considering them to be all a part of the collective bosom of humankind.

The Pluto in Cancer generation possesses both powerful maternal and paternal instincts, which have been extracted from the collective excrement that symbolizes upheaval. Furthermore, the Pluto in Cancer generation are in possession of powerful instincts, which are intuitively guided by their souls. They are, in fact, the quintessential ambassadors for Pluto-orientated transformation.

Pluto Preservation

As we have already discussed, the Pluto in Cancer generation are perhaps the most *vulnerable* to illness and disease. The disease cancer is a particularly prevalent condition that affects this soul group, especially in the breast, stomach, prostate and the colon. Psychologically speaking, these types of cancers occur because this group tend to *evade* personal adjustment, and evolutionary conversion, hence transformation — preferring instead to preserve their rigid ideals.

Furthermore, this group have somehow placed a psychological barrier around them, which is often *immovable*, similar to the protective shell of the crab, only more intensified in density. Essentially, it is this immovable psychological barrier that is the construct for dementia and Parkinson's – conditions that are particularly widespread within this Pluto group.

The overall manifestation of dementia became evermore noticeable during Pluto's sojourn of Capricorn. Therefore, transiting Pluto made an opposition to its natal position in the charts of the Pluto in Cancer generation. This single planetary configuration was most likely the catalyst for dementia, Parkinson's, and of course cancer. Other factors were responsible, such as a square or quincunx from transiting Pluto to Mercury, Saturn or Neptune.

Through my many years of research into the Pluto mechanisms of this soul group, I discovered that approximately ninety percent, and in particular those who had been placed in care homes because of dementia, have undergone some form of upheaval in their childhood. Essentially, dementia represents psychological death and memory loss, hence the preservation of ideals. In other words, they have built a totally resistant barrier towards unsurpassed transformation. Unfortunately, a large percentage of the Pluto in Cancer generation have found it increasingly difficult to adapt to life in the twenty-first century. Dementia is not contagious. However, it will appear to be contagious when there has been a distinct lack of progression in the individual lives of this soul group.

Regrettably, the only way this group is likely to achieve positive soul transformation as an overall collective is when they are literally coerced into it.

Pluto Transformation

Ideally, in order to avoid the prospect of inherent illness and disease, the Pluto in Cancer generation must embrace soul transformation — without the presence of unyielding and underlying fear. Ultimately, they must strive towards the rebirth of the soul by fusing the emotional bodies (solar plexus), with the soul, through the regenerative powers of stillness and meditation. In essence, they must learn to nurture the fragilities that are present within their souls, especially those souls who have been acutely compromised by the preservation of upheaval.

The Pluto in Leo Generation: 1939 – 1957 (Approximate Dates)

The Pluto in Leo generation can be referred to as a magnificent soul group of divaricating proportions. This is because their radiating personalities have the potential to expand, and touch even the most distant of souls – releasing them from the likes of anguish and misery. Above all else, this Pluto group have the collective potential to *heal* the core of the Pluto in Cancer generation. Meanwhile, the Pluto in Leo generation are essentially the cosmic children. To be more precise however, they are known in the Pluto realm of consciousness as the children of evolution. Thus, they have *embraced* the potential to *transform* the lives of others. This evolutionary certainty has been extracted from the relevant files in the *Akashic Records*.

One of the primary tasks connected to this particular group is to transform and nurture their own childlike souls. This will help them *refashion* the collective veil that represents the other Pluto soul groups. This means that they are capable of infusing other soul groups with creative innovation, which will be *consolidated* during Pluto's transit of Virgo. A powerful and psychological transformation, involving this group, would have occurred during the traumatic events of the Second World War – 1939-1945. According to my research into this soul group, many children who were *liberated* from the hands of the Nazis were members of the Pluto in Leo generation. Reflecting further on this notion, a large percentage from this Pluto soul group became immersed in all of the suffering caused by the Second World War. Therefore, they are not averse to the obstructive trappings associated with inherent illness and disease – initiated during adolescence. Individually, the potential is emphasized by hard aspects from Pluto in the natal chart, particularly to the Sun and Saturn.

Exactly how illness and disease manifests, and takes on physical and psychological form, is solely dependent upon the exploitations of the Pluto in Leo individual. So, for example, inborn stubbornness and inbred tension, caused by overwork, can be their curse. Thus, this group has a collective tendency towards working their fingers to the bone so to speak. This is precipitated by the psychological scars of having nothing – reflected by such undertakings as food rationing during the Second World War.

Cardiovascular problems have invariably become an overwhelming issue for this group, especially during the times when they perceive life has indeed *lost* it sweetness, or creativity. A loss of sweetness or creativity would be an extremely difficult concept for the members of this group to comprehend, because the Pluto in Leo soul needs constant and meaningful love and admiration. It is love, and creativity more than anything else, that transforms these souls into greater individual and collective human beings.

Although the Pluto in Leo soul views the potential threat to the health as serious, he or she will nonetheless take it in their stride. However, the innovative sign of Leo has the potential to successfully merge with the Pluto archetype in an auspicious way – creating a confluence of advantageous energy – with the regenerative powers of Pluto. This combination of positive energy is absolutely essential for maintaining good health, and soul transformation. This is because Pluto's sojourn through Leo held the potential to *reawaken* the spiritual heart, which in turn *regenerates* the physical heart. Functioning together in this way, this group represent a source of necessary evolutionary and spiritual development, for other groups to commend.

In addition, those souls who form a crucial part of the Pluto in Leo generation are essentially born leaders. However, despite this positive notion, they are often persecuted by personal doubts and anxieties, which they perceive as irritations. Negative improprieties can impair the overall health of their life force energies, causing heartbreak and other health problems.

The Pluto in Leo generation are also susceptible to spinal (back) problems, particularly in later life, and particularly when they have overworked themselves. This impending circumstance can also occur when moral and psychological support is lacking in their lives. Spinal discomfort can also occur when the Pluto in Leo soul refuses to support others, because they have become immersed in self-pride.

Pluto Preservation

Personal doubts and anxieties are also issues to which the members of this group can easily become *predisposed*. As a result, these souls often bury their doubts deep within the psyche, which causes damage to both the physical and spiritual heart. Self-doubt can also be the root cause of incurring psychological problems, especially in later life. As I pointed out earlier, inherent afflictions that are not contagious become psychologically contagious within each Pluto soul group.

So, for the Pluto in Leo soul group, psychological concerns can result in personal limitations throughout life. However, this group, above all others, tend to fight to the bitter end, especially for the causes they consider to be extremely personal in nature. Some would say that this is their *stubbornness* emerging. However, when they ultimately succeed in their creative endeavours, they will eventually acquire the evolutionary blueprints that determine a successful route towards the transformation of their individual and collective souls.

Pluto Transformation

Ideally, the Pluto in Leo generation must attempt to *fuse* the physical heart with the spiritual heart, in order to acquire love in their lives, and to avoid the prospect of inherent illness and disease. However, for the Pluto in Leo generation, it must be love that is totally *unconditional*, unlike its Sun sign equivalent, which is often dependant. This is deemed as the ultimate amalgamation for this soul group. Thus, to successfully attain personal and evolutionary transformation is no doubt their greatest reward.

The Pluto in Virgo Generation: 1957 – 1972 (Approximate Dates)

The naturally caring and decorous Pluto in Virgo generation have chosen to incarnate at this difficult time in our collective evolution, to necessitate much-needed service to humankind. For the most part, performing service is for the purpose of 'raising awareness.' However, to best describe the concept of raising awareness, is to compound reason (logic) with perception, in the hope of *integrating* the physical and spiritual heart.

Ultimately, raising awareness *will* heal the divisions that exist within the heart of humankind. However, before this Pluto group can orchestrate these admirable measures, they must first *heal* their own souls, by subsequently *increasing* their own levels of self-worth. Healing the divide that exists between the physical and the spiritual heart would essentially be considered as unsurpassed transformation. Essentially, this higher evolutionary purpose is the greatest achievement a soul in human form can achieve. To the Pluto in Virgo generation, this means ultimate perfection. However, if this subtle enterprise is not achieved, the seeds of inherent illness and disease will be firmly set, especially within the psychological framework of this generational soul group.

Overall, this particular group are prone to mental exhaustion, and anxiety — perhaps more than any other of the Pluto soul groups. Principally, when this happens, they become easily distracted, and cannot focus on their primary objective, which is service. So, it is absolutely vital that these souls learn to *silence* the mind, especially through meditation, in order to alleviate these conditions – bringing the opportunity for self-healing. There is an old Arabic proverb, 'silence is golden.' For this group, maintaining this is imperative. They also have the potential to exceed, above the other soul groups, to master Pluto's penchant for psychological transformation.

Functioning with the divine gesture of service will provide these individuals with an evolutionary – of their souls, so to speak. Simply, this is the way they acquire inspiration, and inspiration is the vital ingredient they need to control their inherent attraction towards apprehension and anxiety.

Often, it is not until much later in life that these individuals begin to realize their necessity for self-healing. Psychologically, members of this particular group naturally suffer from a lack of self-assurance, especially within the first half of their existence — leading up to the second Saturn return. However, when Pluto operates from its Virgo station, the generational effects of this planet are *mirrored* alongside the overall characteristics of Saturn. This means that, in most cases, Pluto transformation of the Virgo archetype occurs within the second half of life.

Traditionally, Pluto is in its *fall* in Virgo ; and therefore, its transformational effects can become *suppressed*. The transformation of this soul group will begin in 2008, and through to 2024. From 2008, transiting Pluto begins its sojourn of Saturn-ruled Capricorn – concluding in 2024. Throughout this period, Pluto will make a trine to its position in Virgo in the natal charts of this soul group. This trine will contain healing properties, which will essentially release them from their self-doubt. Once this happens, the need for service will become apparent. For these souls, performing service is a congenital notion. So, when these psychologically connected souls finally accept this inherent challenge, the transformation of their individual souls will be underway. For them, initiating their karmic plan of action is a moment of *exaltation*. Thus, a smile will break out on their otherwise individually bewildered faces.

Although Virgo is a mutable and gentle sign, Pluto, which is the dominant force in this cosmic equation, is a fixed and powerful planet. Therefore, this particular soul group can border on *inflexible*. So, in order that the perfect balance is achieved between these two very different cosmic factions, the Pluto in Virgo generation must learn to surrender to the natural order of life — rather than controlling it. Once they achieve this fine balance, the individual members of the Pluto in Virgo soul group become naturally confident and self-assured.

In a psychological capacity, this group need to be operating at their best at all times. For the Pluto in Virgo generation however, the embodiment of psychological perfection is only attained when the soul finds solace and contentment from deep within their individual souls, which are often acquired via performing service to themselves and others. This is when Pluto and Virgo become the perfect collective alliance.

Pluto Preservation

For the Pluto in Virgo generation, being unable to acquire psychological perfection is often the precursor for mental disorders, as we have previously determined. In addition, individual physical afflictions, which center mostly around the pancreas, can be widespread. Furthermore, gastrointestinal conditions can pose a problem for these souls, becoming psychologically contagious throughout this Pluto soul group.

Currently, psychological illnesses and diseases, such as depression and psychosis are beginning to proliferate. However, most psychological disorders that are prevalent today were starting to be recognized and understood during Pluto's modern transit of Virgo. Thus, the evolutionary transit of Pluto in Virgo, perceived in medical terms, benchmarked a turning point in curative awareness, especially throughout the modern world.

The proliferation of psychologically based illness and disease is perhaps another reason why these souls were ordained to incarnate at this particular point in evolution. Once they confronted their own issues, perhaps they needed to assist in some way with the elimination of this overall psychological disorder. Individually, this conception would be relevant when natal Pluto occupies the sixth, eighth or twelfth house in the individual natal chart. Momentously, the sojourn of Pluto through Virgo symbolized the beginning of the modern medical era.

Pluto Transformation

Ideally, and in order to avoid the onset of illness and disease, the Pluto in Virgo generation must transform their innate sense of insecurity into a deep recognition, one that bolsters their sense of self-importance and reliance on others. Feeling important and being needed are their major requirements, which will successfully activate their inner compass – pointing the way towards self-healing. Once they begin to feel secure within themselves, the collective souls that comprise the Pluto in Virgo generation, become *incumbent* within their individual pursuit towards the service to humankind.

The Pluto in Libra Generation: 1972 – 1984 (Approximate Dates)

For this airy and exquisite generational soul group, the seeds of illness and disease are *continually* sown throughout the course of their life. This is because the colon (Pluto) and the kidneys (Libra) are connected. They are also organs with reproductive abilities; and therefore, they can be a source for concern – continually reproducing the same dis-ease. Thus, the seeds of debilitation are sown deeply into the center of these organs, particularly when there is a distinct lack of personal or collective justice and harmony evident in the individual lives of this 'joined at the hip' collective. In other words, these people become easily *irritated* and *antagonized*, when love is replaced by cruelty. This is because, at the heart level, the Pluto in Libra soul group love everyone and everything. Thus, it is this perceived 'lack of love' that becomes the catalyst for the onset of illness and disease.

Invariably, these souls cannot identify why concern with injustice develops into an ongoing obsession – *blanketing* their otherwise fair-minded personalities. For them, injustice is an abstract notion that resides deep within their souls, and therefore it cannot be processed psychologically. Their perception of injustice is, for the most part, due to the presence of hard aspects to Pluto in the natal chart. To these souls, a lack of harmony represents a major injustice, which the Pluto in Libra generation cannot possibly support or subscribe to.

Pluto is *symbolic* of generational core transformation, whereas Libra is the sign of spiritual equilibrium, and the equipoising of physical matter. Thus, this Pluto in Libra consocation is perhaps best suited to the facilitation of major life-enhancing challenges, which ultimately lead to core transformation, the essential lifeblood of Pluto. This means that the Pluto in Libra generation possess the individual and collective will power to attain soul transformation, by striving to lead the way into bringing the world into perfect balance and harmony. To these souls, this beautiful conception represents the supreme notion of *fairness*.

Striving to bring the world into perfect balance is a difficult endeavour, at the best of times; however, for the Pluto in Libra soul, it can be hazardous. This is because of an innate incapacity for decisiveness. Indecisiveness can be their ultimate vexation – an annoying irritation – and an intense indignation. So, as an elaborate air sign, they can often leave decision making for others to execute on their behalf. This is a fair-minded function that they subconsciously view as being necessary, especially for the transformation of their souls, when indeed it represents nothing more than psychological and physical laziness – something they are accused of on a regular basis.

Notwithstanding, if these souls fail in their quest to transform their souls because of indecision, this *inaction* can also become a precursor for the onset of illness and disease. Indecision (ambivalence) is a psychological concept; therefore, illness and disease manifests initially as a psychological concept. As we have previously established, Pluto rules over the colon, and Libra oversees the kidneys. Both of these physical elements are a major part of the abdominal system. Libran imbalance is created primarily in the kidneys. Conditions such as lumbago and especially kidney disorders are common themes, especially when indecision infects the life of the Pluto in Libra soul. Colon, ovary and bladder disorders can also occur as a result of indecision.

Pluto Preservation

The Pluto in Libra soul group must learn to *detach* themselves from the everyday stresses and strains of life — focusing instead on the everyday joys of life – rather that becoming obsessed by the abstract notion of injustice. However, injustice is a preconceived concept that typifies the seeds of imbalance. Injustice is also a presumption that is incorporated by the absence of truth. However, for this particular soul group, injustice would always prove to be a difficult notion for this collective to resist — even in an ideal world. It is no coincidence however, that they incarnated at a time that signified a mass of global injustices.

One significant example was the cold war between the USA and the Soviet Union (the USSR as it was known then). The USA's purpose on this Earth is to police the world (Pluto), and thus restore harmony (Libra). The purpose of the Soviet Union (modern day Russia) is to restore harmony (Libra) amongst its people, after centuries of indecision (Libra) and intense aggression (Pluto).

The Pluto in Libra generation are naturally *gifted* with an inclination to restore harmony, especially at the global level; this is their inherent ability. Significantly, there are many diplomatic minds on both sides of the USA/Soviet conflict who have Pluto in Libra in their natal charts. They are the souls who aspire towards finding diplomatic and peaceful solutions, thereby *forging* improved relations on both sides of this unending conflict, currently creating global imbalance. Today, the world is about to enter another cold war, because of Russia's invasion of the Ukraine. However, with Pluto about to enter humanitarian Aquarius, this conflict can be resolved much more quickly than previously possible.

To restore balance to the Pluto scales of justice is perhaps a major part of the soul's plan, which has been uniquely designed for this generational assemblage. In addition, striving towards peace, harmony and justice within the confines of these nuclear superpowers (Pluto) is also a major part of their grand plan – instilling peace within the realms of both the individual and collective soul.

Once the Pluto-Libra soul has acquired peace, their internal scales become balanced. Furthermore, the kidneys, and the colon will always remain in perfect harmony with each other. This means that the dialogue between these prolific organs will be nonetheless constant and productive. Talks between these world superpowers, however, will need to be conducted with a constantly productive dialogue, in order to find a resolution. Therefore, I suggest it is left in the capable hands of the Pluto in Libra diplomats.

Pluto Transformation

Not every soul in this group was designated to restore the natural order of the world, especially the disorder caused by global conflicts. Moreover, the fundamental function assigned to the Pluto in Libra individual is to transform their own 'inner conflict' into a genuine, sincere and peaceful accord, which trickles through the soul — an enactment similar to the melodious tones that symbolize the concept of jubilation. So, for the Pluto in Libra soul, jubilation characterizes true harmony, which is the perfect antidote for illness and disease.

The Pluto in Scorpio Generation: 1984 – 1995 (Approximate Dates)

Pluto is Scorpio's ruling planet; this is an exceptionally powerful alliance, because Pluto has developed an immeasurable and intense unanimity with its domiciled and celestial counterpart. Therefore, the *fusing* of these cosmic elements represents a combination of high-powered forces – making them a formidable strength to be reckoned with. However, hard aspects to Pluto in the natal chart can incapacitate the positive effects of this all-powerful alliance drawing attention to attitudes and viewpoints that need to be transformed into something entirely new and purposeful, which is the fundamental purpose of evolution. Hard (frictional) aspects merely *impede* the positive effects of planetary affiliations.

Pluto in Scorpio is a powerful cosmic alliance, which is capable of *strengthening* the physical, psychological and spiritual substructures – unique to the individual soul. These substructures represent the elemental cornerstones of life. Evolution, hence developmental progression, is the foundational purpose of the eighth house in the natal chart, which is Pluto and Scorpio's natural domain. Thus, Pluto, Scorpio, and the eighth house, are the most durable and resilient components in the natal chart.

A friend of mine said that "you could drop a nuclear bomb on those who have Pluto in Scorpio, and they will no doubt survive.[4]" I can see the logic behind this analogy; but, realistically, no one would survive the direct impact of a nuclear bomb. However, with that said, the Pluto in Scorpio generation are an extremely tough and buoyant group of individuals; and they are capable of surviving almost anything that is catapulted their way; particular concerns of a violent and climatic disposition.

The Pluto in Scorpio soul group have incarnated at this point in evolution to *extend* their powerful collective influence, which is to captivate the need for change and survival. They are also here to provide additional power —empowering the evolutionary changes that lie ahead for the whole of humankind – and planet Earth. Therefore, the Pluto in Scorpio generation are perhaps the best equipped group to *absorb* the harshness of these evolutionary transitions, which according to the *Akashic Records* begin in 2025. Supposedly, this is when the golden age of enlightenment is ushered in. Therefore, the Pluto in Scorpio soul group symbolize the embodiment of transformation.

However, this powerful soul affiliation is *not* averse to the dangers associated with physical and psychological afflictions. Therefore, the seeds of illness and disease are invariably planted deep within the individual and collective colon of these individuals.[5] If, at any time, however, they consider that life has betrayed them in any way, or they feel that they have failed in their evolutionary tasks, the colon is the organ that is the first to be afflicted — by the imprecation of indisposition.

The prospect of contracting illness and disease, however, would not *deter* them from carrying out their instinctive and evolutionary obligations. This is because the Pluto in Scorpio generation have literally *invested* their energy into their own individually tailored life plan. This is to 'set in motion' the seed of transformation into the heart of humankind, in order to highlight a more conscious way of existence. For these souls however, failure is a word that is not in their cosmic vocabulary, because failure, or negligence, are convictions they cannot easily assimilate. So, they do not attempt to do so.

While this is true, there are, however, a high percentage of individuals from the Pluto-Scorpio group who are especially *vulnerable* to self-immolation, hence suicide. This represents a specific portion who have Neptune difficultly-aspected in their natal charts – expressly from the Sun, Mars or Saturn. Neptune, is of course, Pluto's mythical brother. So, for them, the concept of self-sacrifice is deeply personal, and it is extremely ingrained. Softer aspects to Neptune, such as a trine from Saturn, or the Sun, would help the individual to develop a more prolific attitude towards death and tragedy, and to a greater extent, more than any of the other Pluto soul groups. Often, they become suicide counsellors as a result.

Scorpio is a fixed water sign; and Pluto is considered to be a fixed water planet. Therefore, this combination of immovable and iron-willed elements can become firmly *anchored* in the psyche. Generally, this means that there is no compromise on what they consider as being *achievable*. Potentially, Pluto in Scorpio represents the perfect synthesis of elements; therefore, Pluto in Scorpio represents the ultimate configuration, especially when attempting to achieve the impossible.

They do, however, have a blind spot. This 'Achilles heel' is an inbuilt desire to be in total control of everything, and at all times. If they feel they are not in control, every measure they undertake becomes a source of disparagement. In some cases, this depreciation becomes detrimental to their overall health.

Prostitution, which is common to the Pluto in Scorpio generation, denotes psychological control over others. Most likely those who have embraced this ancient occupation have experienced deep-set psychological issues, which are mostly brought about by others controlling them. Interestingly, many who make their living in this shady arena of life have Pluto, powerfully placed in the natal chart.

Pluto Preservation

Sexually transmitted diseases, such as HIV, urinary bladder infections, and even depression are potentially common factors for the Pluto in Scorpio generation. In fact, the first recognized case of HIV was in 1981 – three years before the start of this Pluto sojourn. During Pluto's transit of Scorpio, HIV and AIDS were dis-eases that were very much in the public eye. Sex is an extremely important factor for these souls. They often consider this particular act to be a form of power and control – increasing the strength of their overall hot-blooded temperament.

Recently, there has been an increase in the use of the drug ketamine; especially for personal gain. According to a recent survey carried out by the *World Health Organisation* (WHO); the largest group responsible are those in the age group between 25 and 35. This age spectrum is indicative to the Pluto in Scorpio generation. Ketamine is a hallucinogen — providing a sense of self-purpose and sexual euphoria – especially when combined with alcohol. This is particularly prevalent with those who have Neptune badly aspected in their natal charts.

Taking ketamine, however, will *deceive* the anchor-person (reference made earlier to the *fixity* of this generation), into believing they are increasing their overall control, and their sexual prowess. Ultimately, these are the principal reasons why so many from this group indulge in the use of this powerful drug, which was originally used as a formidable anaesthetic for animals, including horses. The habitual use of ketamine has now become indicative of Pluto's preservation hallmark, especially amongst this group.

Another factor, which is *tethered* to the Pluto in Scorpio generation, is to raise awareness towards the dangers associated with nuclear power – a deadly and dark consternation symbolized in the subjective realm of Pluto.

Pluto Transformation

Continuing to raise awareness within these particular domains that represent individual and collective annihilation and elimination, the Pluto in Scorpio soul group are capable of conveying light into their own darkened realm of Pluto — neutralizing the prospect of illness and disease. Encompassing the Pluto archetype with light is symptomatic of evolutionary transformation.

Developing awareness in this way will help the Pluto in Scorpio soul to develop a deeper awareness concerning the dangers that surround their often-obsessive need for power and control, especially in the arena of their sexual activity. Metaphorically speaking, the one principal piece of their anatomy, which they would most likely boast about, is their 'nuclear-powered' sexual organs. After all, HIV is a form of radiation sickness. Moreover, it is these sensitive organs that are always at risk from external diseases. Transformation in this area is therefore required. Alternatively, look at the sexual organs as being the body's external exhaust, hence a necessary outlet that will *channel* their powerful energy.

Meanwhile, for this particular generation, assisted by the Pluto in Sagittarius and Capricorn generations, their conclusive rise to prominence will be a very slow transition. Therefore, the transformation of this soul group will not begin until the second decade of the twenty-first century. Here, their covert work into altering people's perception towards more spiritual matters will come into effect. In addition, the onset of Covid-19 in 2020 will propel this group into fulfilling their ultimate Pluto mission, which is to raise awareness towards the prospect of global annihilation.

The Pluto in Sagittarius Generation: 1995 – 2008 (Approximate Dates)

For the Pluto in Sagittarius generation, evolutionary transformation is established when the soul is finally *liberated* from all of its psychological despair and when the soul has mastered the importance of *responsibility*. Once the soul achieves these difficult objectives the likelihood is that there will be no more illness and disease in the lives of these spiritually-attuned individuals. The Pluto in Sagittarius group are, in effect, the evolutionary *pioneers* of the zodiac.

However, if the Pluto in Sagittarius individual perceives that liberty will never be acquired, the seeds of illness and disease will begin to sprout, mostly in the form of depression. Thus, the Pluto in Sagittarius soul group are particularly prone to depression to a greater extent than all of the other Pluto groups. Sagittarius is the most optimistic sign of the zodiac. Depression, however, lies at the polarity of optimism. Once the Pluto in Sagittarius soul succumbs to depression, the arrows, which they fire *instinctively*, and with a perfect aim, will *miss* their target. Pluto can function as an intermediary between these two opposing characteristics, so that an equilibrium between the two can be found. Once this occurs, the centaur will develop a much better aim for the arrows to target.

The perception of existing entirely within a psychological and physical bubble of *entrapment* is perhaps deemed the worst-case scenario for the Pluto in Sagittarius soul group, but this is the nature of depression. In order to avert this crisis, they need to view their existence within a specific field of vision; one where their three-dimensional compass is operating reliably. This three-dimensional compass is the mechanism that fires their arrows, so it must function at all times.

Subsequently, they need to glimpse their soul's horizon at all times. This is their depth of vision; their main source, which powers their optimism. Furthermore, they can tap into their ancestral power at any given time, which is hidden deep within themselves. In a sense, this represents their breadth of vision. Furthermore, they can share these intuitive powers amongst themselves in a psychogenic capacity. This is their ESP. The Pluto in Sagittarius soul group are the *freethinkers* of the cosmos. They are also the most free-spirited of all the Pluto generational groups. However, they are perhaps the most fragile; therefore, this group are extremely susceptible to a range of mental health disorders.

The only viable way they can overcome the threat of illness and disease is to continually seek inspiration through their wealth of knowledge and evolutionary experience, which they have obtained either in spirit, or in previous incarnations. So, when under the rulership of Sagittarius, Pluto imparts the image of transformation, through the Sagittarian's wisdom of understanding, for the purpose of self-development.

Operating from its Sagittarius station, Pluto's otherwise equable persona will change significantly emerging as rash, hasty, impulsive, and often frivolous in its dealings with other Pluto soul groups, particularly when it involves finance. Pluto is often labelled the *Godfather*, because, speaking metaphorically, when he summons payment on his long-standing accounts, we must take notice. This is a tendency the Pluto in Sagittarius soul tends to overlook, because Sagittarius can be overly generous and flippant. Thus, financial flippancy was very evident, especially within the banking sector, during the latter half of the 1990s when Pluto tenanted Sagittarius.

This reckless period of irresponsibility is more in line with Neptune. However, Pluto's sojourn of Sagittarius marked the beginning of an era where ill-considered and senseless banking came to the forefront in many countries. This was an inadvertent period where banks *freely* released money without carrying out credit searches. Money was more-or-less given away in the form of loans, credit cards and mortgages to bad debtors, low earners and students – those who are ordinarily considered as high-risk categories – pigeonholed because of financial risk or inexperience. Thus, an impending global financial collapse was inevitable, expected during Pluto's tenure of Saturn ruled Capricorn.

Ironically, from 1995 and through to 2008 marked the period when depression began to proliferate. Although depression has always been around, its modern-day seeds were initially sown during Pluto's sojourn of Scorpio. Furthermore, a recent study conducted by the *World Health Organisation* (WHO) concluded that those who are most susceptible to the onset of 'monetary depression' were between the ages of 17 and 25. Further studies concluded that the vast majority of students in higher education (Sagittarius) were succumbing to this form of depression, because they were running up colossal and catastrophic bank overdrafts. This was also the time when student grants were abolished in favour of bank loans.

For this particular group, being financially and psychologically *damaged* is perhaps the worst form of entrapment, because it is *inescapable*.

Pluto Preservation

Sciatica, which is an underlying and enervating health condition caused primarily by inflammation of the sciatic nerve, is a very painful and debilitating infirmity. Thus, the origins of sciatica are often deeply-ingrained in the body's physical DNA sequencing, congenital patterns that are evolutionary by design. However, speaking in a psychological capacity, sciatica is often a consequence of financial distress, which is equally responsible for the onset of physical entrapment. Thus, sciatica is common amongst the Pluto in Sagittarius generation.

The Pluto in Sagittarius generation are also predisposed to diverticulitis, which is a very debilitating chronic condition affecting the entire length of the colon. For this generation, the colon is symbolized by the Sagittarian arrow – carried by the mythical centaur of Sagittarius. However, for this Pluto embodiment, diverticulitis is caused, in part, by a *dissipation* of life's eternal sweetness (optimism).

Meanwhile, all financial concerns contained within the mindsets of this evolutionary grouping, will be finally addressed once Pluto's sojourn of Aquarius begins in 2024. In addition, these apprehensions will be purged once Jupiter (the ruler of Sagittarius) links to Uranus (the ruler of Aquarius) via a sextile in 2022. Thus, the Pluto in Sagittarius generation will be given an opportunity to finally *shake off* their financial burdens, particularly with those academic students from this group.

Pluto Transformation

Sagittarian idealism, coupled with Pluto's transformation, can be a forerunner for necessary change. Differing and diverse experiences are what drive these souls in their quest for knowledge. Furthermore, when experience is fused with knowledge, evolutionary growth can be achieved, at which point the Pluto in Sagittarius generation can transform into 'beacons for hope' – a point in which illness and disease are finally eradicated. Ultimately, this marks the evolutionary nature of Pluto's sojourn in freedom loving Sagittarius.

In order to limit and restrain their rash and hasty behaviour, I would suggest courses in mindfulness, and regular sessions in heart-centered stillness. These gentle disciplines are both recommended for preventing and overcoming illness and disease. When stillness (peace) is applied to the psychological mindset and the physical body, the heart becomes free and is no longer subject to entrapment. Once the heart is free, the scope of these individuals' philosophical beliefs becomes simply fathomless.

The Pluto in Sagittarius generation are the teachers of life's eternal knowledge. Thus, they are here to *pave* a new direction for the entire world to follow.

The Pluto in Capricorn Generation: 2008 – 2024 (Approximate Dates)

Because this evolutionary timeline was *paralleling* the compilation of this book, my analysis of Pluto will extend only to the salient points, thus fusing together these cosmic hierarchies.

For this Pluto group, the seeds of illness and disease are 'karmically sown' when its individuals fail to achieve, or refuse to recognize, their predestined obligations and responsibilities, which are *imprinted* upon their souls. Hence, the predestined responsibilities of the Pluto in Capricorn generation are directed towards an indispensable need for accountability. This means that they must always be accountable for their actions. For them karma is swift and apparent – unlike, for example, the Pluto in Pisces generation – who, in most cases, must wait until passing into spirit before karma is applied.

In addition, their predestined responsibilities mean to instil level-headedness within the overall collective influence, at this time of great physical and psychological upheaval upon the Earth plane. Thus, they are in a sense here to restore a sense of *composure* amongst the rest of humankind.

Furthermore, the ultimate preservation of new world structures and foundations are also crucial factors of recognition for this group. In other words, they have incarnated to build, restore, and protect the infrastructure for the new world order. A further assignment for them to undertake is to ensure that the rest of humankind remain in complete control, especially during this period when chaos and upheaval reign supreme. Global turmoil will become paramount during Pluto's final transition of Capricorn, which is representative of the final decan of the sign, 20 through 29 degrees respectively. Moreover, global chaos and uncertainty will be personified when Pluto makes an evolutionary conjunction to Jupiter and Saturn in 2020.

During Pluto's final transition of Capricorn, the world will witness the threat of global annihilation, caused in part by pandemic, power control and systemic globalization. It is therefore the karmic duty of these Pluto-Capricorn souls to bring these concerns to the forefront, so that a long-term solution can be found, and before Pluto's absolute evolutionary transit of Aquarius – beginning in 2024.

Interestingly, when Russia, a country ruled by Capricorn (see chart), invaded Ukraine in 2022, many of the student humanitarian aid workers, and those who were attempting to seek a long-term solution to the crisis, have Pluto in Capricorn. Research also shows that some have Venus in humanitarian Aquarius. Those souls who have Venus in Aquarius in the natal chart will excel when Pluto enters Aquarius because Venus is at the natural polarity of Pluto.

In effect, the Pluto in Capricorn generation have ingrained in their souls a moral duty of care and responsibility to themselves and others. They also have a responsibility to the Earth. In effect, they are overseers of the truth, and the abolishers of corruption. They also have the added benefit of *time* on their side. Psychologically speaking, for the Pluto in Capricorn soul group, they have all the time in the world to put things right.

Pluto Preservation

Pluto's position in Capricorn initializes the onset of illness and disease, via the outer layer (skin) of the colon, commonly referred to as the gastrointestinal wall. Diseases that affect the skin of the colon include colitis, gastritis and ileitis.

Depending on the strength and condition of aspects to Pluto in the individual natal chart, the Pluto in Capricorn generation are particularly susceptible to diseases concerning the outer layers of the bone, known as the cortical bone (skin). These include the progressive disease melorheostosis, which seriously inhibits the bone's natural development preventing the evolutionary transformation of the soul. Stillness and meditation are crucial which these souls need to undertake. Essentially, Pluto in Capricorn is showing us that the skeletal infrastructure of the Earth has also become diseased.

Pluto Transformation

For all of us, further advancements, which result in technological and evolutionary rewards, such as medical breakthroughs, are there for the offering, especially when we consciously agree to *raise* our current evolutionary awareness. Altering the course of our current direction must become essential, especially when Pluto finally departs Capricorn in 2024. In order to achieve this transformational shift in psychological consciousness, we, as a collective, will have to transfer our collective perspective from the darkness of negative thinking, and towards the light of positive reckoning. Most notably, this is concerned with the transformation of individual and collective awareness.

Evolutionary Transformation

For the moment, the transformation of the Earth, and all its inhabitants will hopefully begin to move forward — towards an anticipative period of reckoning and serenity. Thus, the notion, and the fallout from illness and disease, should begin to subside as we traverse further and more significantly towards 2067. At that point, everything will become a disturbing, but nonetheless distant memory. 2067 is the year that Pluto begins a wholly new evolutionary cycle of the zodiac – beginning in innovative Aries.

The futuristic Pluto generations, namely Aquarius and Pisces, will be able to *reposition* the cosmic spotlight of optimism and hope, over the current gloomy notion of despair. However, the abolition of illness and disease will only become possible if the Earth isn't impelled into cataclysm, for a seventh time in its evolution.[6] Thus, as Pluto completes its cycle of the zodiac and moves towards zero degrees of Aries (an anaretic degree),[7] the opportunity for the regeneration of the Earth, and for humankind becomes a realistic (Aries), and evolutionary prospect (Pluto). I, for one, remain hopeful of this necessary and ultimate transformation.

Furthermore, as ignorance and greed are gradually *purged* from the Earth, primarily by the generational effects of Pluto's sojourn of Aquarius and Pisces, individual and collective unity, enlightenment and awareness begins to increase both exponentially and internally. Moreover, during this forthcoming cyclic era, where the future generations begin to remember their spiritual heritage, and which denotes the cycle of the philosopher's wheel, humankind is being re-awakened to the possibility of telepathy, telekinesis and self-healing. Unfortunately, these spiritual and fundamental characteristics were *overlooked*, and mostly *ignored* during the evolutionary period which was designated as the dark night of the soul.

Let us now briefly examine Pluto's sojourns of Aquarius and Pisces cultivating their salient points of reference.

Pluto in Aquarius

As we have already ascertained, Pluto is the planet of transformation and regeneration. Aquarius, however, is the sign of psychological and spiritual progression and innovation. Conceivably, this temporary cosmic collaboration has the potential to be advantageous, if absolute transformation is the desired objective for the individual and the collective mindset.

Once Pluto begins its lengthy transit of this sign, life, in all its dissimilarities, will gradually become *antiquated*. Thus, Pluto's transit of Aquarius characterizes a glorious opportunity for humankind to make some preferred and necessary changes to the collective influence, as well as our own individual lifestyles. In addition, this evolutionary transit symbolizes the dawning of the age of the scientific revolution. Hence, the scientific revolution also distinguishes a prolonged period of observational transformation, meaning that we will be given a period of time in which we can contemplate the purpose of our existences.

Collectively speaking, we have already experienced a small portion of this approaching transformational epoch coming to pass in early 2020, earmarking the beginning of the Covid-19 pandemic; 2020 was the start of the scientific revolution. Thus, the scientific revolution is now very much at the forefront of our existences. For now, until roughly 2043, we will begin to witness a myriad of scientific breakthroughs and major successes, particularly where medicine is concerned. Changes to the law, and social reforms could also be on the cosmic agenda, and there will be an abundance of new ideas, particularly surrounding the colonization of space, although I doubt whether this will amount to anything tangible. After all, Pluto is attempting to transform our ideas and beliefs away from this notion, concentrating instead on the wellbeing of our Earth and its inhabitants.

Pluto's penchant for death and transformation to the spirit world began to *spiral* throughout and 2021, with the Covid-19 pandemic. However, those scientific Aquarian brains, which have become very attached to the scientific revolution, created the vaccines, which were meant to inhibit the transmission and deaths associated with Covid-19. Equally, and as with all scientific developments, there are always going to be the 'Aquarian-labelled' conspiracy theorists. We should, then, expect a monumental surge in this type of behaviour distorting the balance of the scientific revolution when Pluto begins its sojourn of Aquarius in 2024.

Quantum leaps within the scientific community will nevertheless continue and become a prevalent factor all through Pluto's tenure of Aquarius, providing we hold our 'collective nerve,' so to speak. Pluto's initial entry into Aquarius has the potential to be a problematic and undependable transition, causing further unrest and distrust in the world – until Pluto discovers its grounding at approximately eight degrees of Aquarius – eight denoting awareness in fixed signs.

Science should, however, continue to discover vital cures for some of the world's deadly diseases. I wouldn't be surprised if a cure for HIV and AIDS (Pluto) isn't finally discovered during this time. It all depends on our undivided ability to *raise* our collective vibration (awareness), as Aquarius demands.

If we can manage to pull off such feats of accomplishment it would be considered as a monumental achievement, especially within the realm of ecological and biological diversity, which fall under the rulership of Uranus, the natural ruler of Aquarius. What is not considered, or even understood by the media, is that deadly diseases not only cause damage to humans, but they also harm the Earth's ecosystem. During Pluto's tenure of Aquarius, we finally have a chance to *repair*, and further *protect* the environment.

Humankind will be presented with an opportunity to alleviate disease, once and for all. What an accomplishment that would be; a timely enterprise for when Pluto commences its journey through the Godly sign of Pisces. Ultimately, Pluto in Pisces marks the final journey, bringing to an end this modern evolutionary cycle for the planet of transformation and regeneration.

Pluto in Pisces

Pluto transits the sign in which his mythical brother Neptune rules. Previously, when Pluto tenanted Pisces; hence 1797 through to 1823, above all else, it embodied the secret age of inquisition, and 'illegal' witch trials. These illicit proceedings still take place in some parts of the world today – secretly functioning throughout the annals of time. In America, witch trials officially ended in 1693, but in parts of the UK for example, women are still being ostracized for their so-called harridan beliefs. For the most part, these secret practices have transpired since Neptune (secrets) began its sojourn of Pisces in 2011 – its rulership sign. Pisces symbolizes the sign of the witch; it is also the sign of the healer. Mostly, witches were healers; who were unlawfully misconstrued as being immoral (Neptune). Thus, in my opinion, the age of inquisition is still very much alive.

However, when Pluto enters Pisces in 2044, the age of inquisition will either be reinforced, or it will be dissolved, once and for all. With that said, when Pluto enters Pisces in 2044, humankind will be presented with an illustrious opportunity to forgive for all those former provocations, cruelties and grievances. *Finally*, during this transit, the seat of humankind will be able to *release* the distant memories of all these historical wrongdoings. In essence, this transit will symbolize the dawning of the age of idealism, spiritual regression and higher reasoning. Anyone born during this Pluto cycle, will be collectively known as the *Children of Tama*. According to the *Akashic Records*, Tama means 'excessive augmentation.'

Moreover, this fathomless cycle will symbolize an evolutionary period where doubt, fear, pain, suffering, and all of those negative emotions, which have prevented us from progressing as individuals, and as a collective for millennia, can be relinquished forever. However, as always, human beings will be faced with a choice. Either we can move forward in an enlightened and spiritual way, and with the health of the Earth at heart, or we can continue to regress, as we have done so for thousands of years. During Pluto's sojourn of

Pisces, humans can *spiral* further down into more obsessive addictions. Furthermore, human beings can continue to pollute the Earth – increasing the deleterious effects of global warming.

If we choose the latter option, the Earth will be the subject of a cataclysm; at which point, humankind will be eradicated. According to the *Akashic Records,* this will be the seventh time, and will involve the element of water. Pluto, Pisces, and its ruler, Neptune, are all cosmic components symbolizing the water element. In addition, cataclysm will occur during Pluto's tenure of Pisces, because the ruler of Pisces, Neptune, equates to a seven in numerology; and this will be the seventh time. Alternatively, we can choose another option; and that is to learn to love ourselves, and the natural environment. As always, the choice is ours!

Let us hope that Pluto's tenure of Pisces uplifts our spirits, and stimulates our creative imaginations, and our hopes and wishes.

In Conclusion

If, and this is a very big If, humankind *survives* its current, and its future challenges, it is inevitable that the Earth will be a very different place around, and certainly long after 2067. This evolutionary amelioration would nevertheless symbolize the natural healing of the Earth, and the Pluto collective world order.

Blessings to you, the Dear Reader

                                                Alan Richards-Wheatcroft

Chart Data:

Natal Chart for Charles Darwin, 12th February 1809, 15:00 GMT, Shrewsbury, UK, Placidus Houses, Mean Node.

Natural Chart for Nicholas Winton, May 19th, 1909, London, Mean Node.

Mundane Chart for Russia, 25th December 1991, 17:25 MSK, Moscow, Placidus Houses, Mean Node.

References

[1] Information source Wikipedia.

[2] The age of enlightenment is followed by the golden age of enlightenment, beginning in 2043. This information is in accordance with the Akashic Records.

[3] According to the Akashic Records, the illusion known as the 'acceleration of time theory' initially began in the year 2000. This was the year when the Earth's energy grid was increased to 96 decibels. This increase in energy output was put into place to assist with the major changes that are continuing to occur upon the Earth plane. Since then, our traditional concept of time has been transformed somewhat, because time appears to be accelerating.

[4] A reference to the astrologer, John Dawson.

[5] The colon is scientifically deemed as the secondary memory core.

[6] Drawn from the Akashic Records.

[7] Anaretic is a term used for critical degrees. This 29th degree of any sign is deemed as a crisis-orientated point in the chart. Some astrologers have interpreted an anaretic degree as meaning that a point has been reached in mastering an important lesson in the universe, but success has not quite been achieved as a result.

CHAPTER ONE

Pluto in the Trajectory of Human History

"One of Pluto's greatest anxieties is not being in control, and it is concerned about how to survive in any given situation."

The Astrology Place

We know that Pluto takes 248 years to orbit the Sun, spending on average 20 years in each zodiac sign. We also know that Pluto is retrograde for about 160 days each year. Hence, the very slow motion of Pluto symbolically gives us a considerable time frame to detect and eliminate any feelings of guilt we may have, toxic discernments, or unethical principles that could negatively affect us as entities, organizations, or as a society. Consequently, Pluto seems to have both a personal and a collective resonance, despite its classification as an outer planet.

Moreover, Pluto resembles the destructive and regenerating force, the death stage of the life. That which, symbolically speaking, Pluto can't regenerate or transform, will be slowly eliminated from our reality. Pluto doesn't represent just one thing; it represents an entire package that we all have accumulated in our own way over time. Consequently, Pluto eliminates things from our existence gradually, by burning them one by one, and the process is very intense and notable.

The ashes that remain behind could represent a symbol of who we really are as an entity The way we choose to be on Earth and how we burn our energy daily will have some impact on our soul. Nevertheless, because Pluto is moving very slowly, it likely means that we may not have the time to end one full cycle in one lifetime; the meaning of Pluto seems to point out a particular segment of life; what we have to redefine, regenerate and transform in this incarnation. Apparently, Pluto may be perceived as secret conducts, channels through which we can carry some meaningful concepts, a collective package that may help to gradually redefine the human evolution. One generation is connected to another through these unseen cables. It will be in the obscure cables, symbolically, in a secret manner.

The power of our World is not only represented by the richest, the most powerful politicians, people who control the other human beings; it is represented by oil, atomic energy, the wealth of minerals, and the roots of our heritage as human beings on the plane of the Earth. Perhaps the authoritative power cannot be left in the hands of everyone, it must be controlled, protected, especially if this type of influent energy can have an impact on the collective level. What is naturally hidden usually may have value and power. Without discovering the keys of the natural treasures of the world, we as nations, social organizations, or human beings, are not powerful, not even rich enough.

At an individual level, the real power in my concept does not represent just the perfect form of human realization; it is the one that we can't buy, it's the inner power that we generate slowly, after a long time of burning layer by layer of challenges that allows us to reach the center of our soul and have internal transformation. Therefore, the real power of our World is the collective energy, the positive social vibration that can grow plants, and create ideas; that can heal the pollution, negativity, and move the world in the sense of progress and evolution.

In other words, the invisible wires could be so strongly connected throughout our planet (countries, continents); they may represent the earth roots that may vitalize the future of human development. The group we belong to protects us, and we know how to protect our environment in the way we are. In fact, the constitution of any country is a national consciousness codified. Nevertheless, the fundamental laws of the earth must reflect the psychology of the people, ideologies, the influence of religions, and the political and legal cultures. All of them in some way dictate the power that controls the world's population to a point; I call this man-made or hand-made power.

The rest of it is a mystery and requires training to be understood, a supreme power, that might come from different, profound forms of life experiences. Consequently, without any crisis moments of life or mysterious impacts, I am afraid that we are not capable of understanding the full path of human nature.

However, what if those invisible wires are affected by germs, a negative power that could poison the truth of some group activities, or even redirect that human handmade power? What if negative influences can slowly cause damage to some roots, and therefore the premature death of some important connections among continents, countries, or leaders of the world? So, from the start this could be just one example of how the power of Pluto can be split between positive and negative, stimulating either group with either slow, constructive intentions or the ones with destructive, dictatorial purposes. In this context, the concept of bad is not subjective, because we use it as a base for the morality of humankind and simple humankind morality can't be contested. None of the leaders of an unhealthy or a corrupt organization can redefine the morality in their interest because the moral sense is already well-defined by our consciousness. We just need to work on discovering it.

Going forward, symbolically, as an individual influence, Pluto investigates each layer of our soul. It controls each movement of our existence, in order to create a solid, uncorrupted foundation for our future. It will restart or reprogram us as many times is necessary in order to progress powerfully, without any inappropriate complicity or harm to our soul root. Moreover, it will let us see the layers of society and it will invite us progressively to gradually discover each one. However, secretly, our soul seems to be planted in a particular community and at the same time protected by a hidden power. We as human beings are the richest entities on this planet, symbolically, the wealth of minerals and gems found on the earth ground.

Perhaps, using Pluto symbols, we are like stones and our duties are to transform ourselves into a powerful energy that may grow not just the self-root, but also the roots of our community, to be part of and to support the progressive movement of the Earth. When our individual feelings can create such energy, then we, as human beings might become a generator of light that can detect any shadow in the world. Our human inner mechanism seems to be able to enact such a mystical process of total transformation. Nevertheless, we will be moved to find any truth covered in mystery shadows, in darkness.

Innate Energies

We all have a *mine* inside and all of us have a sense of feelings. To activate our profound energy, we might have to break many times and in a very exhausting way, in order to contact the self-human stone, the individual gems. Eventually, we may have to become ash or a powder to be able to easily fly and to be converted into a new human role. In other words, we might have to pass an intense human test, that I call a spirit purification. People and society in general with a history of suffering and crises may acknowledge that the dominant force came after caring and comprehending the individual life challenge package.

The best group resolution does not come from books; it comes from wisdom. Hence, our capacity to accumulate pressure and transform it at the same time in a positive vibe may fully define our spirit. Some of the most influential, powerful and wealthiest people in the world have demonstrated that they could redefine themselves no matter what. None of the life tests were so hard that they could not be reborn or reinvent and redefine themselves. However, it seems like only those who did not go over the limits of morality could reach the mystery power. In this sense, we might have to find the energy to work obsessively with ourselves and develop our passions. These will always awake our inner energy, and it might place us on the avenue of our destiny.

The vibration that we have created in time could represent the sensors of our body, and they seem to be valuable life tools for each one of us. In some cases, there is a superior power, one that can play or even control death; a force that can also move destinies. Here, I can enumerate some of drastic life changes, such as adoptions, near-death experiences, life relocations etc. It's like the power of the Universe may have a job opening and subsequently, a particular soul has been chosen to do a specific task, a particular service to humanity. In most of the cases, the meaning of this type of regeneration could not be understood at the same time as the actions developed. The rhythm of a very cruel life will unfold the suffering and once accepted and burned , it could define a clear meaning that may even elevate that soul, may empower the force of that human being.

As you can perceive, there is a contradiction here. Pluto usually has low vibrations, or at least may drive us to the point where our life's waves coming to an end. We may even literally die; or we maybe get that boost from the very bottom, and have such a total conversion that can even send us to the top, to acompletely new environment, or who knows, to start a new life path. Here's a simple example: imagine someone that takes a plant from its original place and puts it in another pot, for better nurturing, vitalization and growth. Concealed influences may come from outside to redefine life principles and to implement a healthy routine.

Despite all of the healthy or beneficial outside resources, our inner force makes the final decision; our inside power must make a mystery connection inside us that can reboot our energy, that can recognize the inner potential, and give us a second chance. It's like our inner energy must light up every cell of our body. So, symbolically, Pluto regulates and controls the outside environment, where we are stuck most of our lives, and gives us time to research inner elements that could empower our identity in the world. In other words, Pluto can be seen as 'the bodyguard of our soul.' He will protect us from outside, but it may let us burn inside, feeling and figuring out the answers to so many WHYS. For instance: Why some specific wish that I have had for years is not coming true? Why do I have to wait so long for something that others can get very easily? There seems to be a distance between our needs and our possibilities to achieve those needs. This distance could be exactly the time that the soul needs for self-redefinition.

The emotions that we have created inside us as individuals or as a society might be burned and transformed into energy. There seems to be just one powerful energy, and we humans must choose how we want to manifest it: positively or negatively. Also, we control the intensity, as individuals, depending on how powerful the existential sum of the spirit is. What about a society or a country? Could it be more powerful just because a group of highly evolved spirits are living there or are leading the community? Is the world we have created, the world we deserve?

Going forward, we know that Pluto is manifested the best in its own environment, the sign Scorpio, that is known as the most intuitive, insightful, and secretive. I always perceive Scorpio as "one step forward and two steps back".

'Under Scorpio influences, the person may not hurry to navigate into the future until the past is well understood."

Perhaps being the first sign from Libra, Scorpio knows well

how to balance things, and perhaps, for this reason, cannot proceed quickly with its own (passion) enthusiasm, and always looks back for feelings of confirmation. Maybe it's not about melancholic actions; it may be about being cautious , or maybe it is about waiting for the intuition to unfold or approve the next step. In this sense, intuition is like a pipe, invisible veins inside of which people may put their own feelings, to research and to work for their interest. Symbolically, Pluto on its platform seems to make a correlation between the past and future; between the outer world (Universe) and our world, what you see and what you don't see; between our value stones, and our Universe to which we belong. In other words, we all are particles from the Universe. Perhaps our duties are to discover the mysterious part of the life, the dark or invisible world, and then to mark it in such a way of abstract beauty, to be able to see and understand the art around us, the art of life. In fact, many writers have affirmed that the art is the higher form of spirit manifestation.

Art is an expression of thoughts, emotions, and inner pressures that have been collected over prior existences. Each of us can create art and transform the life platform in an art workshop, where you work with passion, determination and very intensely. You may like to create a colorful, outstanding picture, for generations to recognize a second from an old-time; a gift to your soul to take as a souvenir as it starts a new existence; a heritage for your spirit. In fact, our world is a beautiful creation of art. We see and understand this art in the way we, as human beings, have developed universal principles. Over time, we may have to adjust our spirit to different life principles that may correlate to a different generation.

However, the mystery of life, the secret, consists in not going too far or too fast and staying with the natural rhythm of the spirit, the same harmony with nature and the Universal rules. Any other method of navigation through life could be an unhealthy one and it might turn us back to the point of Pluto regenerations. Neptune is the planet before Pluto, and Neptune represents boundaries ; a highly artistic soul may break the boundaries to reach out to the zone of secret power. In this sense, perhaps only a highly spiritual soul may have that 'easy pass' to navigate towards mysticism.

Pluto in transit brings powerful influences to the area and the degree involved in the transit. Pluto will zoom out, on average, about four to five areas of a person's life: it will evaluate and re-evaluate that area of the natal chart. Perhaps those areas in the chart are in the end the most important of the actual incarnation. Perhaps it marks the direction for gradual progress and evolution, and it depends on each one of us to be able to connect and synchronize with it. The world around us will influence us in a manner that could gradually transform our deep human sense. Moreover, regarding charts for countries, an average of four to five sections will be the most important zones to be re-evaluated for one generation. In other words, that segment may represent the areas where that country might have to work intensely in order to regenerate its supremacy, eventually to implement ethics that could redefine its principles. Hence, it is very important to watch Pluto, not just in annual individual transits, but also, in the long-term astrological reports of individuals and countries. It always points to the zone of an activated volcano, and it might indicate long-term intensity.

Volcanoes have tipping points, which manifest as eruptions. It will be very interesting to analyse that point in the charts of countries or the influential persons that control the world through their social decisions. We can comprehend this zone in detail, just allowing our passion to understand the aspects that hold that pressure. Who is on the dance floor, and what dancing style do they have? It seems to be a mystery, how the invisible could become visible, especially when Pluto, symbolically speaking, has to dance with other planets like Saturn. The dance styles might be different than others because there seems to be a dark energy that could not allow the rhythm of the world vibrations from manifesting naturally. Each one may control the steps and each of them may want to manage that style of the dance. Consequently, what is not pleasant may increase the perception of the duration of time, so the dance between such planets could be so long and unpleasant. However, it's important who is assisting! Lot of times we do things carefully and with respect just-thinking about our interest or our reputations.

In his investigation, Pluto cooperates with other planets, symbolically, researching details about our subconscious condition, our identity in the world, creation, capacity to act, life principles, our limits and how far we can go with our reality. It may trigger major changes; in order to see more and expand the quality of life, many of us navigate towards visions. Pluto will look to detect the most precious point of someone's soul, it might break down doors, and it might break through the unseen walls to get closer to that mine. Nevertheless, it will recognize and amplify the worthy soul. I have found that Pluto in major negative aspects with other planets could be very difficult to hold and consequences might appear, especially if there is a tight conjunction. Consequently, such a non-understanding inner energy may degenerate into very negative, destructive actions. However, this is not an excuse, and we should not assume that Pluto wants to bring destruction. Pluto wants to empower us, but his strength can only be held, metaphorically speaking, in our hands when we are capable of keeping it intact, in non-abusive ways, despite any life circumstances, and in a way that does not harm or affect others.

On the other hand, none of the planets work alone. We analyze them individually to better understand their qualities, but the planets are like musical instruments. We know how each of them sounds, but the orchestra can create a unique song each time. So, Pluto, like other planets must be integrated in regard to the specifics of each chart and must be analyzed based on that chart's particularities, for better understanding. Do you know what your inner song sounds like?

Symbolically, Pluto could represent the low key, but the

one who has an imposing sound. It reminds me of the sound of church bells. In Christianity, when somebody from a community dies, the church bells ring to spread the news. Inevitably, when we describe Pluto, we may want to include that form of something cold happening in society, another death in time, hence frozen time. It may not be frozen, but because of our incapacity to unfreeze/ resolve social issues it could be defined as an impossibility, an issue that we conserve and pass on to the next generation. Going forward there is a difference between Pluto's influences in the natal chart and the ones in the transits chart. In the natal chart, Pluto unfolds layer by layer from exterior to interior, until we gradually discover our inner secrets, our soul.

In addition, Pluto will invite us to participate in cycles of time, to experience and understand the natal aspects that it forms with other planets. Consequently, it lets us decide how profound we want to go, to comprehend the circumstances, or to play the game of life. In contrast, in transits, Pluto's influences are progressive; it will move us profoundly from where we are in time to another point. Secretly, it pinpoints our life avenue that we have to stay on, and eventually reconstructs it. I said reconstruct because we are tempted to repeat the same mistakes over and over. We may abandon one way of discomfort and may start a new direction, unaware that the same lesson will come again but under a different form. Therefore, in transits, Pluto wants to elevate our life experiences. Pluto doesn't ruin our life; it may guide us and control our power until we will find the evolution point, the right direction. Additionally, Pluto is heavy in its influence, and it will make us press the button of our change.

Consequently, when we think about Pluto's attributes, automatically we may have to take into consideration Pluto's complicity. In fact, all the personal planets and social planets in transit will pass through Pluto's natal position. The winds of life will blow us through it to confront our existential challenges. No matter how many times we may try to navigate through it in other ways, thinking we can do it because we are an exception, unfortunately, we cannot go around it. There seems not to be an excuse, an exception in this regard. So, Pluto sifts everything so well, and then, allows us time to act in the way of self-transformation, or a social transformation (if is about countries). It's like we might have to go under an X-ray machine to scan each bone of our skeleton, or the soul must be viewed with a magnifying glass, multiple times and from different angles. Nothing can be hidden forever. It brings to mind the popular expression, which is, the truth always comes to light.

So, Pluto may symbolize that profound truth that was laid inside our soul, during the times of each incarnation. Some of us will even try to control the hidden idea of the truth, but the idea of having secrets is to understand what we hide. If there is something that may benefit a group or a society, it may be useful to liberate our soul. Even if we are part of a certain generation, recognized by Pluto in a particular sign, Pluto will be personalized in every natal chart. It will form unique aspects, supported by others, such as pattern aspects. So, Pluto will have progressively a different tension, created by a specific generation and its tendencies. In collaboration with other planets, Pluto might symbolically try to control the circumstances to achieve more for us.

As a result, we as an entity will slowly incorporate into our character the meaning of total change, the idea of who we are at one point and who we can become over time. Imagine life with its circumstances, with the outer elements influencing the inner world, the soul in one specific direction. Then, imagine we could transform all these circumstances into colors. There are so many of them, so many variations of colors and different shadows. Then, imagine how we could renovate our inner self, our souls in a unique way! The interior side of our spirit could have so many colors, so many memories, reflected just in the combination of colors. What type of soul are you in terms of colors? Are you an abstract one? Inspirational? There are so many variations, and they all are unique.

In my view, with each incarnation we have an opportunity to renovate, to paint our existential story. Moreover, as we already know, each painter has his/her own style created in time. Perhaps, each soul has outlined its own style, which could or could not be defined, but there is always a possibility to adjust, to correct or balance the color of our existence. The aspects between planets are a blend of various energies, a mix of colors. Each planet has a color. What color is your soul?

CHAPTER TWO

Pluto in Complicity with Other Planets

"Pluto's position in the natal chart is the place we experience our personal tragedy, and where we feel the least in control."

The Astrology Place

General View and Examples

Any natal chart contains information at a very rich level, hence the project of one existence. It contains or reflects in full detail the skeleton of one's existence. In this equation, Pluto has a crucial role in our evolution. However, to perceive Pluto at a higher level in a specific chart, it must first be integrated into its platform and understand its role in that environment. Generally, Pluto's aspects are hard even if it is about major positive or major negative.

The difference is the manner in which we know how to deal with these influences. The quality of the final result depends on how we have overcome each round of influences as we gradually unravel the mysteries of some situations. Therefore, the house where Pluto is located in the natal chart is the starting point of mastering the challenge of another existence.

Pluto in Collaboration with the Moon

This particular configuration seems to be the most *personal* and *intense* one of all, as it describes our strong needs that are evaluated monthly. By transit, The Moon passes through both transiting Pluto and natal Pluto each month. That day could be intense emotionally, especially if there are natal planets around that point. Also, a deep connection with past feelings may appear regarding the house Pluto is transiting. It could be an unfortunate memory that may follow the personal emotions. Symbolically, Pluto profoundly analyzes our subconscious, feelings, and habits. It may eliminate things from us each month that could gradually create a moody attitude, even building personal frustrations.

The intensity of an aspect between Pluto and the Moon always will be in rapport with the Moon phase under which the entity was born. For instance, a person born under the New Moon will have a different life approach to a particular challenging situation than a person born under the Balsamic Phase. In the natal chart, Pluto, in collaboration with the Moon, may give us details about our consciousness. How profoundly does it affect us overall? It may investigate each layer of our subconscious. Is there a dead layer of feelings that you neglected to overcome? Is there a habit that you forgot to use? Is there a frozen sentiment? Are you stuck in a profound emotion state that makes you very secretive and introverted? Hence, exploring Pluto in connection to the Moon is the first step in recognizing intense emotions. In my view, the Moon symbolically collects the complexity of our emotions that we have generated during the day, while Pluto tries to comprehend, to investigate the circumstances, and transform them. There could be a sense of discomfort, but our inner force can control the energy that we bring inside our wheel. For this reason, we might need to train our resistance, self-control, instincts, and emotions. Consequently, Pluto-Moon collaboration must be balanced. Otherwise, things could escalate in such negative ways.

Perhaps then, there is no coincidence that the Moon is the ruler of the first water sign and second cardinal sign, with negative polarity. We can generate negative emotions that could cause us to take action, initiate things. Sometimes, Pluto-Moon energy may induce denial, feelings of not easily accepting influences from the outside world. This could funnel into us a very cold and unstable energy. The Moon unravels our needs, the type of security we need, while Pluto is power, domination, obsession, sex, and control. If this mix of energy is not well understood or integrated beneficially in our life it could damage our subconscious.

Examples in this direction could be an emotional attachment to the wrong person, being emotionally manipulated by negative influences, groups or having passion for bad habits. This could create an intense inner conflict where our soul refuses to regenerate and revitalize its power. Perhaps this is one of the reasons why Pluto in conjunction or hard aspect to the Moon may also show depression. In other words, Pluto may symbolically sever something that is deeply attached to our subconscious that has not been observed. Any emotional detachment, for example, could be noticed and also be felt at an emotional level and not necessarily in terms of external objects, things that can be recognized by the eye.

Examples of Pluto in Collaboration with the Moon

Juan Garcia Ábrego

Juan Garcia Abrego is a former Mexican drug lord who started out his criminal career under the tutelage of his uncle Juan Nepomuceno Guerra (the former head of a criminal dynasty along the Mexico–United States border now called the Gulf Cartel). He has Pluto conjunct the Moon in the first house, in the sign of Leo. In this equation, the Sun is important because it symbolically coordinates the energy of Pluto and the Moon.

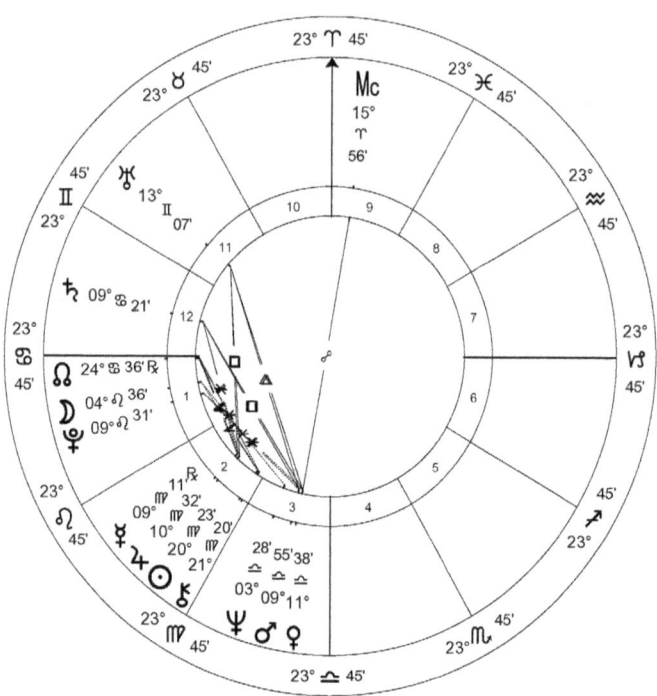

Chart 1: Juan Garcia Abrego; September 13, 1944, 2:00 AM; Matamoros, Mexico

However, Sun conjunct Chiron (in Virgo), in the second house emphasized his approach to making money and growing his financial status. It seems that Chiron is quite influential. Moreover, we know that Chiron shows how and where we can become leaders and teachers, rather than followers. Additionally, he was born under the Third Quarter Lunar Phase which outlines the idea of his emotional maturity and capacity to develop future actions. However, the key to his authority and power in the world is represented exactly by this conjunction of the Moon and Pluto, because just these two, along with MC, are in the fire element. Moon in Leo conjunct Pluto shows an obsession with his needs and to the ability to become an important leader.

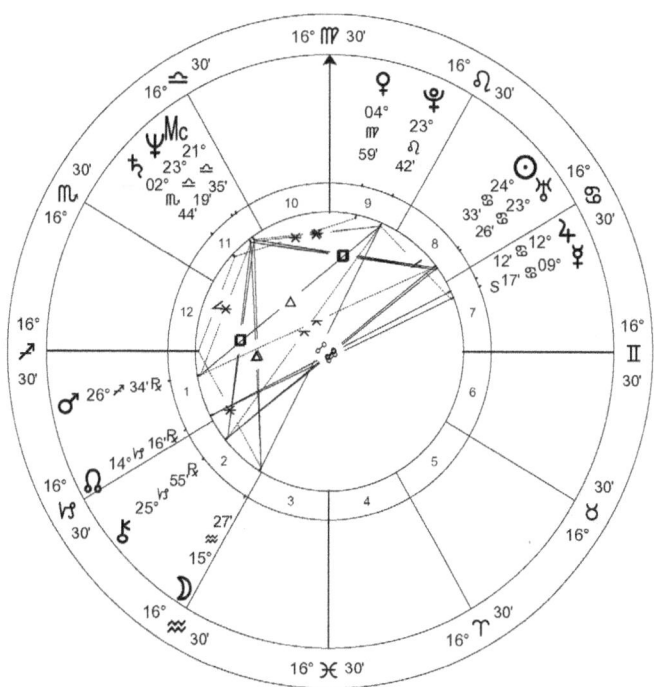

Chart 2: Angela Merkel; July 17, 1954, 6:00 PM; Hamburg, Germany

Moreover, the Moon is the ruler of the chart, but does not work alone since it is conjunct Pluto, indicating a lot of manipulative emotions and controlling energy.

Angela Merkel

Angela Merkel is a German politician who served as as Chancellor of Germany from 2005 to December 2021. Merkel has been widely described as the most powerful woman in the world and "Leader of the free world". She has Pluto in Leo (ninth) opposite the Moon in Aquarius (second). She was born under the Full Moon in Aquarius which emphasizes her need to cooperate and to participate in humanitarian actions. However, her needs may be in divergence with her power in the world. The Moon may periodically bring challenges to Pluto with respect to everything that is represented by the ninth house: foreign countries, politics, philosophy, law, etc. Also, Pluto (9th) is trine Mars in Sagittarius (1st). This aspect could be an important key to the chart because both of them represent the bases that support her future vocation. Pluto and Mars are part of a Minor Grand Trine, where Neptune is the focal planet. Moreover, Neptune is conjunct MC in Libra (11th) and Libra is associated with diplomacy. Hence, we can comprehend her ideals, the idea to search for perfection, because we know what elements from her chart support her vocation, her public manifestation.

Because of other important aspects and aspect patterns in her natal chart, this minor grand trine seems to be hidden in the chart, but it is more important than we think. It may bring extra opportunity for active realization. Additionally, Pluto and Mars are the only planets in the fire element, so her inner drive may work constructively to control things. Hence, this aspect supports her political intentions and her role of bringing equilibrium to things that are in fire or war zones. She seems to be a naturally good mediator who may sacrifice her personal dreams in favor of the big ideals of society.

Viktor Yanukovych

Viktor Yanukovich is a Ukrainian politician, and the former President of Ukraine. He was orphaned as a teenager and also, he was imprisoned at age 18. His natal Pluto (11th) in Leo is square the Moon (8th) in Taurus. He was born under the Third Quarter Moon Phase which may allow him to put his knowledge into action. However, his emotions could be challenged by everything that is associated with the eighth house, including death, the afterlife, heritage, hidden relationships, and money belonging to others. Periodically he could have felt intense pressure caused by his emotions and memories. His needs could have been defined in terms of security, money, sensual pleasure, and physical

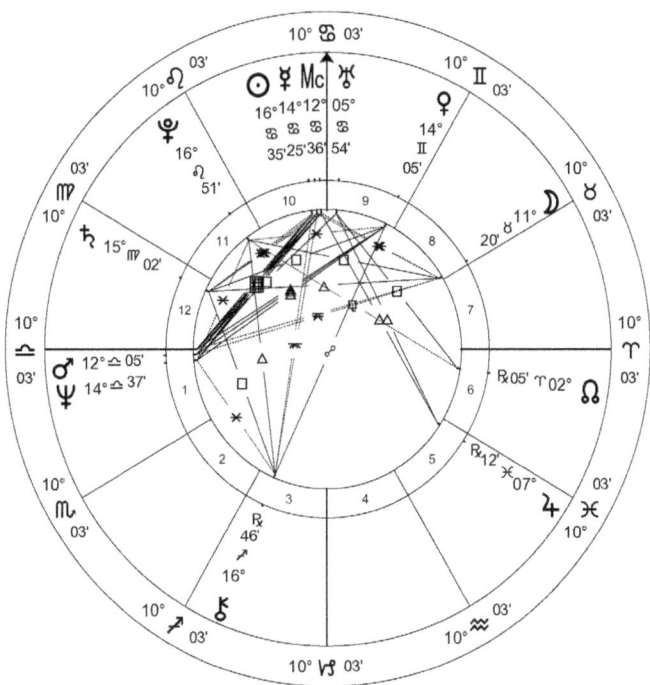

Chart 3: Viktor Yanukovych; July 9, 1950, 12:15 PM; Jenakijevo, UA

comfort. The Moon is in Venus's sign and Venus is the ruler of the chart. Moreover, Pluto is sextile Venus (9th) and Neptune (1st). Pluto is the focal point of the pattern aspect Minor Grand Trine which may open extra opportunities to his future actions. Additionally, Pluto trines Chiron (third) in Sagittarius both of them being the only two planets located in the fire element. This offers us valuable information, in terms of how he connected with the sense of confidence, power and authority.

Lady Gaga

Lady Gaga is an American singer, songwriter and actress. Her self-expression could be defined by the conjunction be-

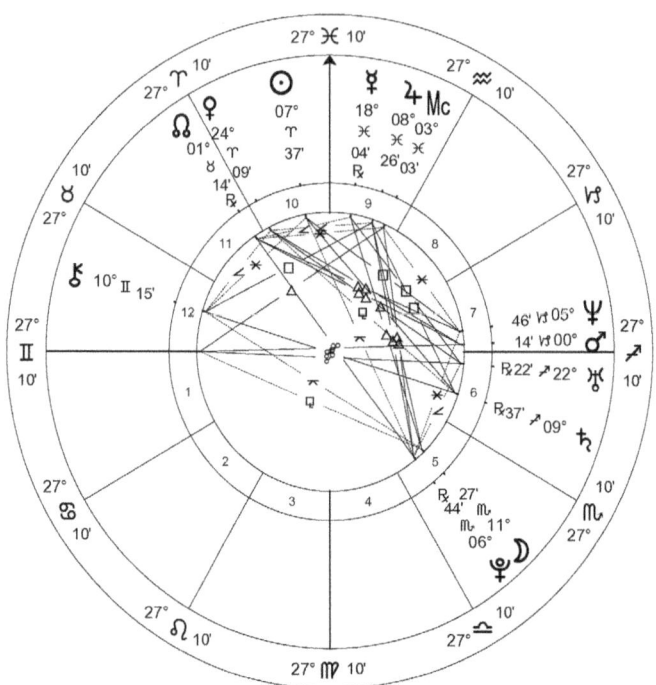

Chart 4 Lady Gaga; March 28, 1986, 9:53 AM; Manhattan, New York

tween Pluto and the Moon in the fifth house in Scorpio. This conjunction seems to make her so profound, hence her inner intensity and self-mastery may have helped her to create such popularity!

She was born under the Full Moon Phase; the Moon is the planet signifying popularity and being in the fifth house explains her preference during her free time for expressing her emotions and feelings. She seems to have crisis skills and the power to change what she doesn't see as truthful. Moreover, Pluto trines Jupiter (ninth) in Pisces, conjunct the MC. Therefore, Jupiter is in his own sign, and is supported by powerful Pluto (also in his own sign) in achieving her lifetime goal. Jupiter magnifies everything, and I believe Lady Gaga might have other tremendous goals that she wants to achieve in the future. Additionally, Pluto sextiles Neptune (seventh) in Capricorn. So, even if Pluto is conjunct the Moon, Pluto also forms a pattern aspect, a Minor Grand Trine, where each of the planet involved has an important role: Jupiter is conjunct the MC in Pisces (ninth) and Neptune is the focal point of this Minor Grand Trine, in the seventh (her relationship with others).

Pluto in Collaboration with the Sun

Pluto in collaboration with the Sun may give us details about our life force and vitality, about our real identity in the world. This type of aspect might shape our character considerably. It might give us a sense of what we are in the process of becoming. It may strain our individuality and eventually it might provide us with the power to develop our hidden creativity.

Generally, as a first step, perhaps the most important one is to recognize the power of our uniqueness, to fully understand our inner authority and self-confidence. We might need to have that vision to recognize our path and play with our originality. If we ignore it, the rejection might gradually create negative energy, reflected in our ego, such as powerful vengeance. Theoretically, Pluto, in connection with the Sun influenced by negative energy could empower potentially negative leadership (a dictator) or could stimulate negative, secret actions.

By contrast, individual motivations could be secure, and the person may emphasize the masculine principles or the image of a hero in his environment, society, etc. Pluto in connection to the Sun can be such a powerful and positive aspect. Usually, the Sun brings light to darkness, and Pluto seems to need the most light to warm up the abilities of humankind, even to manage hidden things. It emphasizes the natural power of leadership, the power to control others talents, uniqueness, to stimulate others activities, to see and comprehend things even if they are in the dark,

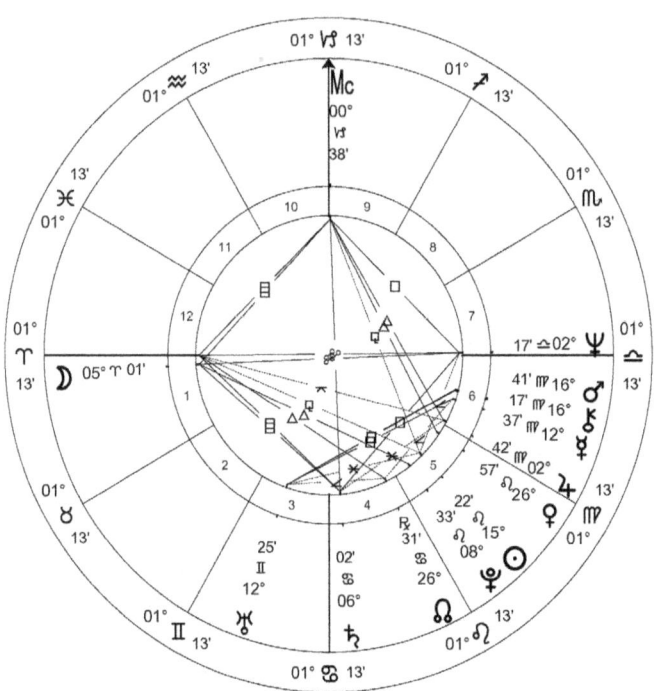

Chart 5: Robert Mueller; August 7, 1944, time unknown; New York, New York

and to moderate any coldness. The Sun can vitalize or give life to any corner of our souls.

Examples of Pluto in Collaboration with the Sun

Robert Mueller

Robert Mueller is the former Special Counsel for the United States Department of Justice and American FBI chief. We don't know his time of birth; therefore, we'll ignore the position of the houses in this example. However, the natal chart shows that he has Pluto conjunct Sun in Leo. He was born under the Sun's sign, so the Sun has a distinctive importance in his chart. However, the Sun is conjunct Pluto automatically creates mixed energy, so we have to analyze both of the planets, together. Briefly, this aspect shows natural abilities to lead, control, and have full power to develop his plans. Pluto is about the underworld, crime, terrorism, sewers, drains, and money as power. So, he could have a natural drive towards detecting these dark activities, to bring to light unseen scenes. Nevertheless, the Sun in his sign highlights the necessity to have independent actions.Moreover, he was born under the Disseminating Lunar Phase which lets us know he would like to share information based on his experiences. More than that, his chart emphasizes the earth element which makes him very tactical, reliable, practical, and efficient with a strong sense of detail. So, the base of the chart supports his powerful identity in the world.

Henry James

Henry James is an American writer of short stories and novels, noted as one of America's great novelists, writing novels such as: *The Bostonians*, *The Ambassadors* and the *The Golden Bowl*. Pluto is conjunct the Sun and Mercury in the 8th house, the house of sharing with others. This is one of his quotes: "We work in the dark - we do what we can - we give what we have. Our doubt is our passion and our passion is our task. The rest is the madness of Art." Notice how many words that are associated with Pluto are used here: dark, passion, doubt. These quotes describe very well Pluto conjunct the Sun and Mercury in the 8th house. How has Henry James described so well an aspect that is very preeminent in his natal chart ? Was he into astrology?

As you can see, he has a Stellium in Aries in the 8th house, which is the house of Pluto, traditionally speaking. What amazed me the most is his Moon, which is in Pluto's sign, Scorpio, in the 3rd house, the house of writing, even short writing, short trips, letters, education, and is also the house of siblings. He was the brother of psychologist-author William James. The Moon is about our subconscious and psychology. Additionally, Pluto

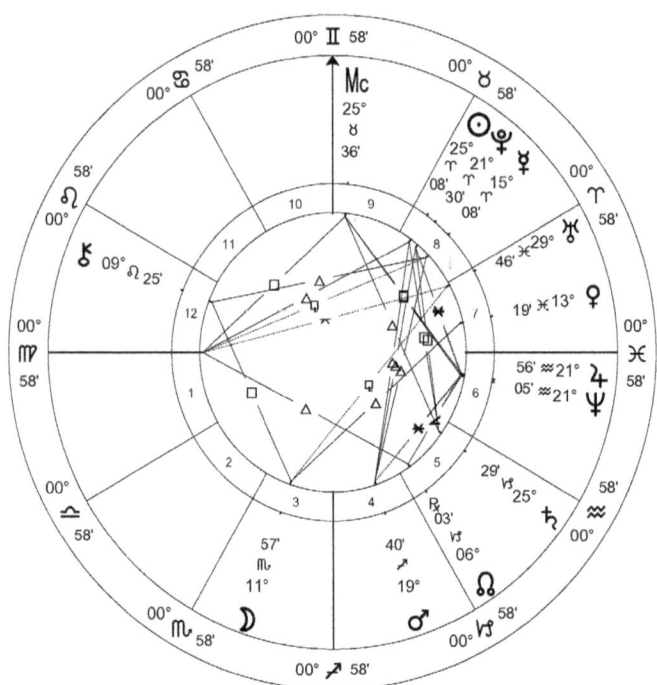

Chart 6: *Henry James; April 15, 2:00 PM; New York, New York*

is part of a pattern aspect, The Minor Grand Trine, where the focal point is Jupiter conjunct Neptune in Aquarius (6th). This aspect brings extra opportunity for the progressive realization of the potential ease and enjoyment; and highlights his extensive knowledge and self-satisfaction for social work. Also, Jupiter and Neptune are in mutual reception to Uranus, emphasizing his eccentric work that is dedicated to others, to change and transform.

Larry King

Larry King was an American talk show host, radio personality and columnist, the host of the world's most potent talk show "Larry King Live"; on CNN TV. King's audience is global and

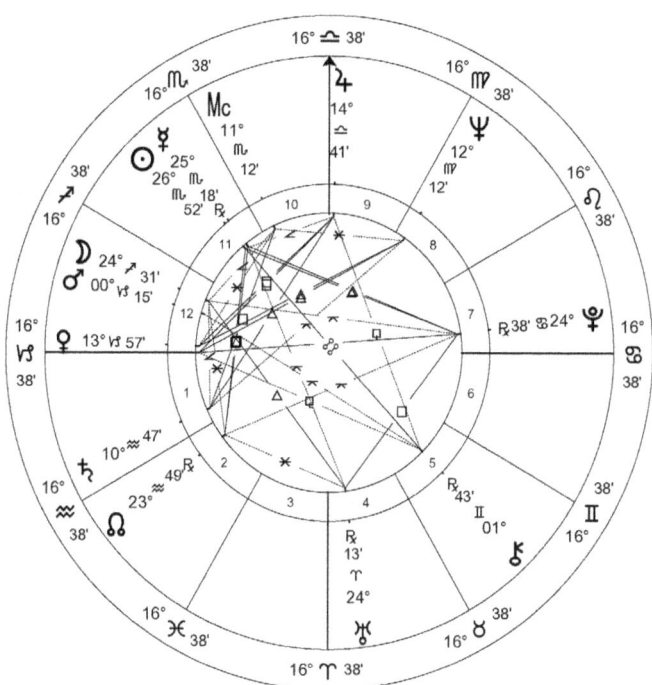

*Chart 7, Larry King; November 19, 1933, 10:38 AM;
Brooklyn, New York*

he is the author of several books.

He has Pluto in Cancer (7th) trine both Sun and Mercury in Scorpio, (11th), Pluto's sign. Also, we know that the 7th house is the house of others, and Cancer is the sign of popularity, initiation, while the 11th house is the house of worldwide reach, international friends and common dreams. These planets - Sun, Mercury and Pluto- are the only planets in the water element, highlighting the type of his attachment and the zone from where it came; how he uses his creativity and his mind; how he is connected emotionally to others, and what type of regeneration he may bring to his broad group. Nevertheless, he seems to have power to dominate and control others mentally. Despite Plu-

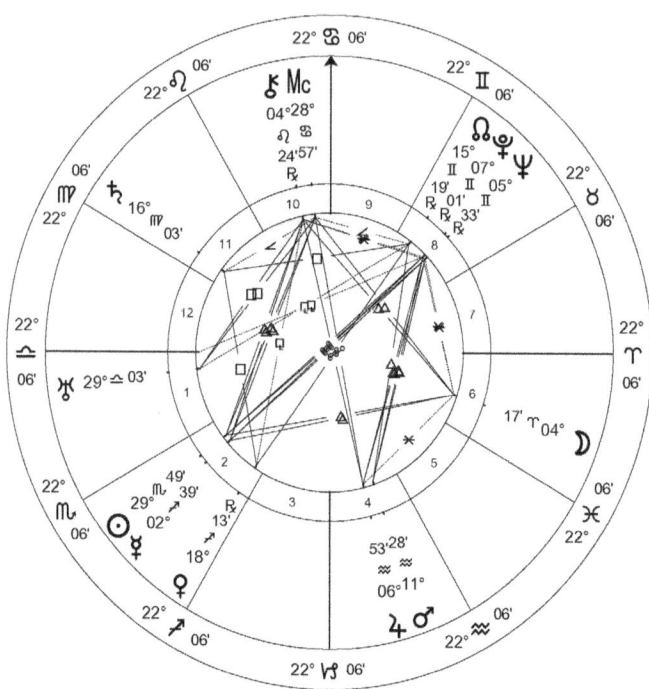

Chart 8: Charles DeGaulle; November 22, 1890, 4:00 AM; Lille, France

to's positive aspects, Larry King's natal chart shows that Pluto squares Uranus. This aspect may challenge his high intellect, eccentricity, or his approach to social media.

Charles De Gaulle

Charles DeGaulle was a French General and politician, a national hero who was elected as the first President of the Fifth Republic from 1959-1969. Pluto is in Gemini, (8th) opposite Sun in Scorpio (2nd), and also, opposite Mercury in Sagittarius (2nd). These aspects emphasize many contradictions and crisis moments over time. His individuality, his plans, could have been limited and controlled by others. Also, his quest for truth or faith messages could have been compromised and transformed many times.

However, Pluto conjunct Neptune may accentuate the importance of the group vision, the regeneration of a social ideal despite his own thought or personal ideals. He seems to have had the intellectual power and the determination and strong dignity to bring transformation to his generation.

Pluto in Collaboration with Mercury

The mixed energy of Pluto and Mercury can burrow into the minds of people and activate an in-depth perception; they might perceive more than most people can do. This energy may provoke a person to understand the thought process, the mental functions, to comprehend and detect each layer of the human intellect. Many profound thinkers who have been fascinated with the human psyche may have had Pluto in aspect with Mercury. Traditionally, Mercury is known as the messenger of the gods. So, there could be an obsession in terms of connections, words, thoughts, ideas, plans, language, or other forms of communication, such as a connection to the other side. Hence, Pluto-Mercury collaboration may show a powerful ability, a magnetic attraction to understanding the most challenging minds, even researching and investigating the criminal ones. Nevertheless, it emphasizes an agile mind with a instinctive curiosity about death, researching and spying. It may highlight a passion for knowledge, and a determination to discover details about how others process information.

On the other hand, Pluto is slow and quiet; it does not use too many words. However, Pluto's strengths are intuition and observing feelings and sounds that could be perceived and translated into words. Imagine that you are in a basement, and you hear slow water drops. You don't see where the leak is coming from, but you listen to it, you use your capacity of perception. The people on the street, those who pass by that basement will not hear the noise, unlike those inside and closer to

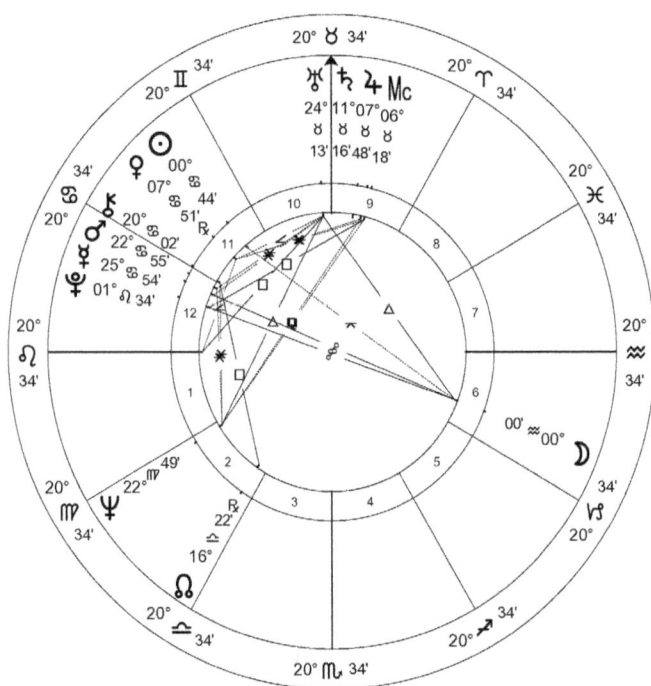

Chart 9: Charles Harvey; June 22, 1940, 9:16 AM; Little Bookham, England

that water leak who will. In that room, in the dark, with those repetitive leaks, you might be determined to imagine many things; either it's a broken pipe, or a flood or other details related to that subterranean subject. So, perhaps we, as human beings, need to be connected, close and ready to use our intuition channel, to follow our instincts, the instructions of our inner drive.

Mercury works the same in combination with Pluto. Some people can also understand what is behind other's minds, under the layers of different realities; they may intuit the unseen or not allowed, unknown things.

Examples of Pluto in Collaboration with Mercury

Charles Harvey

Charles Harvey was a British astrologer, teacher, author, researcher and counsellor. He earned his diploma from the Faculty of Astrological Studies. First of all, his chart shows an imbalance of elements. Pluto is the only planet in the fire element. Also, the air element is missing. However, Pluto (12th) conjunct Mercury might have complemented his character. Perhaps it could have brought confident energy, passion for knowledge which could help him create a mystery connection to the abstract world. He could have a long inner process of transformation, where he put his intuition and emotions in action to initiate lengthy projects that might help him and others understand things behind reality, even the human psyche, helping others to heal themselves and transform their social ideals.

As you can see, Pluto is part of a water Stellium (11th), and also opposite the Moon in Capricorn (6th) which suggests that he may have struggled with detachment, emotions, and elements that could have linked him to real life, including habits. However, his chart highlights a Kite pattern aspect, that contains a Grand Trine in earth (Uranus/9th, -Neptune/1st - Moon/6th) with a focal point in water, accentuated by a Stellium (Mercury conjunct Pluto, Mars, Chiron).

Volodymyr Zelensky

Volodymyr Zelensky is a Ukrainian politician, screenwriter, actor, comedian, and director who was elected President of Ukraine on 20 May 2019. First of all, he has his Ascendant in Gemini, so Mercury (Capricorn, 7th) rules his natal chart, emphasizing the importance of communication and having stable connections and secure relationships. However, his process of thinking and his informative system could have been periodically under crises, transformation, and regeneration. Pluto in

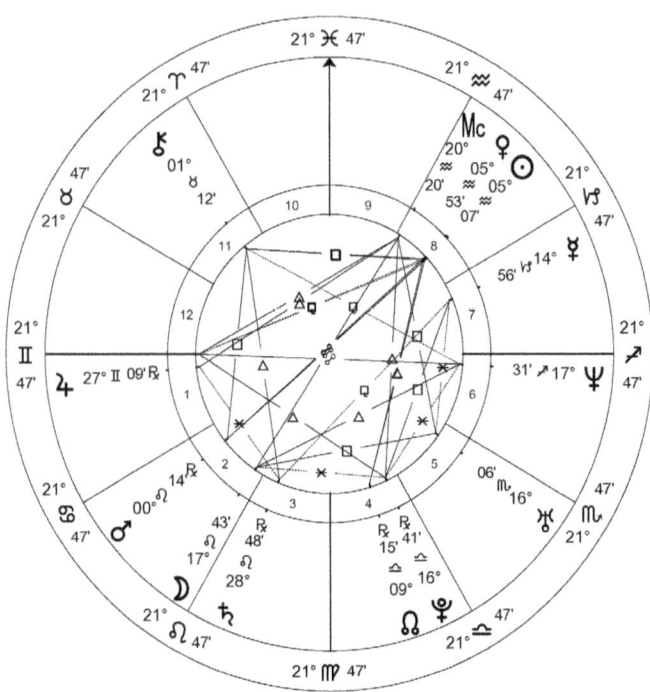

Chart 10: Volodymyr Zelensky; January 25, 1978, 2:00 PM; Krivoj Rog, UA

Libra (4th) squares Mercury; it's a Cardinal square, which indicates initiations. Moreover, Pluto is the focal point of The Minor Grand Trine, in which Pluto sextiles both the Moon (2nd) and Neptune (6th). This aspect shows extra opportunity to bring realization in terms of the 4th, 2nd, and 6th houses.

However, Pluto in the 4th represents not just our inner temple or our parental house; it represents our natal country, too. Volodymyr, being the president of his country, might have an important redefinition to it. Additionally, he was born under the Full Moon in Leo, which gives us details about his private needs, respectively: personal heart connections, loyalty, giving and seeking approval, and taking risks for excitement.

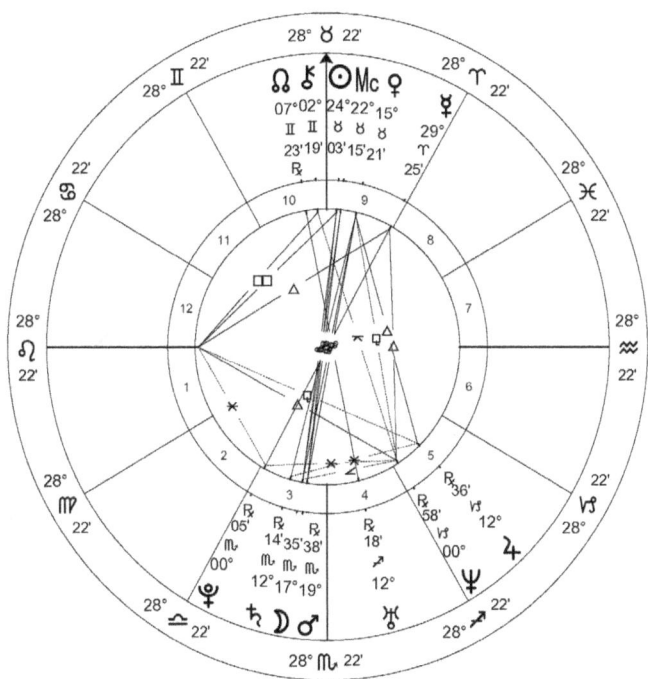

Chart 11: Mark Zuckeerburg; May 14, 1984, time unknown; White Plains, New York

Mark Zuckerberg

Mark Zuckerburg is an American computer programmer and co-founder of the social networking site, Facebook. Even though we don't know his time of birth, his natal chart shows Pluto in Scorpio opposite Mercury in Aries; symbolically this might periodically require adjustment in terms of his intellect and passion, how he handles knowledge and how he controls social information.

Mercury is important in his chart because it is the ruler of the North Node, the point in the chart associated with future patterns and life's directions. The way he unfolds Mercury principles shows us his sense of destiny, the way he will evolve

Pluto: The Power of Transformation 31

and find new paths. Moreover, he was born under the Gibbous Moon Phase which shows us how important it is for him to express his opinions. Additionally, Mercury is the only traditional planet in the fire element, and none of the planets are in air signs. Also, Mercury is the ruler of one air sign, Gemini, which deals with communication, so it may add another slight importance to his chart equations. As you can see, Pluto will challenge Mercury periodically, practically, putting his thoughts, ideas, relationships, and connections in conflict, creating difficulties, inorder to rebirth his intellectual concepts and plans; to become objective.

Pluto in Collaboration with Venus

Venus represents our artistic perception, how we see beauty, and what we find aesthetically appealing, while Pluto represents passion and obsession. In combination, they represent artistic passion, mysterious creativity, and the art of profound love, of living in a permanent state of transformation, to reach the inner peace, respectively 'the perfection.' Also, this combination might detail the capacity of unconditional love, a profound affection no matter the circumstances. Moreover, it might show how well we are connected with the values of humanity. As long as we are related to human values, we may determine the intensity of our transformation, life's tests. The difficulty appears in rapport with the life values of that spirit. Pluto conjunct Venus might create a deep platform of experiences in terms of love, people, relationships, values, and money. For instance, you may love your environment, but the expertise that you may have might send you out of your social cycle; later, when you eventually come back, you better understand the values of that society. In other words, you might start out with just your own values, and come back with your values transformed. Pluto will dissolve the meaning of attachment, may change your affection, and could bring up pure love from the shadow, no matter the circumstances.

After many years, you might have different perspectives,

different ways to see things, perhaps because you have already renewed and stabilized your life principles; Nevertheless, you could experience a purer form of love. With this renewed set of life's principles, you could be like a magnet for your environment, but you could understand it's too small for you to live around just those values. Hence, you are out and in, because Venus is a personal planet and Pluto an outer planet. You could be the person who connects these two zones, the early environment and the external world.

On the other hand, not understanding when you must redefine or nurture that love may create an obsession for a person or social value. In regard to this type of love, there may be destructive energy, jealousy, and an obsessive control over the loved one. A negative example, in this case, is the famous athlete Oscar Pistorius. He was convicted of the murder of his model girlfriend Reeva Steenkamp. He has Pluto conjunct Venus and Mercury in Scorpio.

Examples of Pluto in Collaboration with Venus

Joyce Carol Oates

Joyce Carol Oates is an American novelist, poet, critic, essayist and librettist. One of the most versatile writers of her generation, Oates authored more than 90 books by the year 2000. She is also a creative writing professor at Princeton University

She mentioned in one of her interviews: "The basis of art is conflict" She has Pluto conjunct Venus in Cancer on the cusp of the 6th house (1° orb), and Pluto opposite the Moon in Capricorn. She also mentioned that she lived in Detroit (1967), just two blocks away from the area where shots were fired. She has

Pluto in the 6th house, associated with everyday routine. Pluto may describe negative power: gangsters, the destructive world, and the advanced idea of war. Also, she talked very often

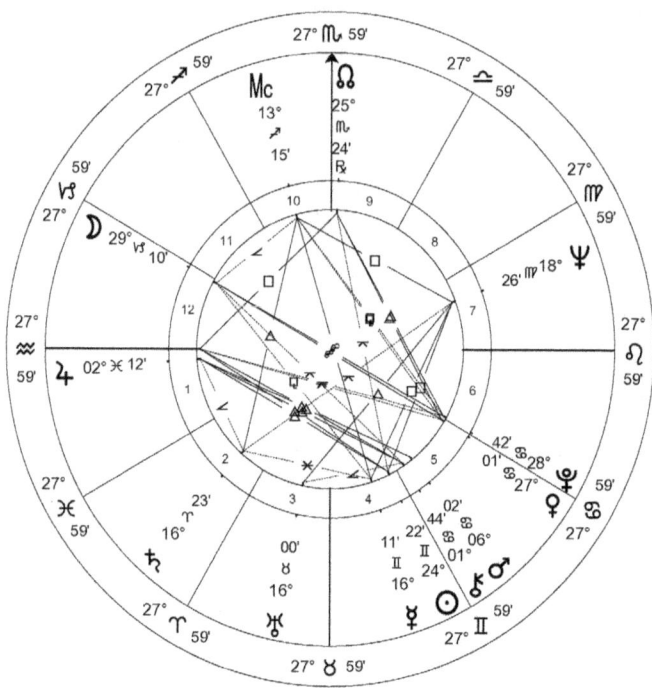

Chart 12: *Joyce Carol Oates; June 16, 1938, 0:27 AM; Lockport, New York.*

about emotions as the basis of her thoughts and how she perceives reality. The basis of her work, primarily, is her capacity to deeply comprehend collective affection, love, and everyday routine as human. In her book, *The Faith of a Writer: Life, Craft, Art*, she mentions her forbidden passion, and talks about deep emotions that may come from deep experiences. In the same book she includes a very interesting phrase: "the writer's first thought is I have to tell". Because the Pluto/Venus conjunction is in Cancer, a cardinal sign, there may an emphasis on initiation.

Venus is such a supreme planet, a planet that offers something essential for humanity. It offers us peace; it can relax people in such a way as to enhance profound creativity and beauty. Art is the higher expression of the human spirit [1]. Art represents the way we communicate with one another and writing is an example of an art and craft. She used her profound energy in her work in such a way that she was able to publish many books. Moreover, as a base and support of her existence, she has the element of Water emphasized in her natal chart; emotions would have been familiar to her.

However, an important component of her life experience is Pluto opposite the Moon which could have challenged many times her feelings of security, her memories, her basic needs, and the unconscious. In this way she has translated her feelings, making them public. Cancer is the Moon's sign, and the Moon represents popularity and public response; consequently, for Oates, Pluto conjunct Venus is influenced by the Moon as well.

Virginia Woolf

Virginia Woolf was a British author, considered to be one of the most important 20th-century modernist authors. Her natal chart shows Pluto in Taurus (12th) trine Venus in Capricorn (8th). Despite the earth trine, Pluto works under Venus's principles. Pluto represents the tiny, heavy tools lost somewhere in our existence; that we must discover and integrate somehow into a group, or into a society. Her Pluto is in the 12th house, which indicates that symbolically her power could have been controlled and contained within an obscure, private zone. The secret place where she could escape or be isolated could be defined by tense energy, depression, and a negative atmosphere.

However, exactly those types of inner experiences could have forced her to navigate further in life by transforming her reality into a new spiritual identity. Of course, during her spiritual transformation she seems to have had realistic and valuable support, especially from the mystical zone, including the occult, death and heritage. In this case, Pluto and Venus cannot totally define or describe her life. In fact, none of the aspects worked

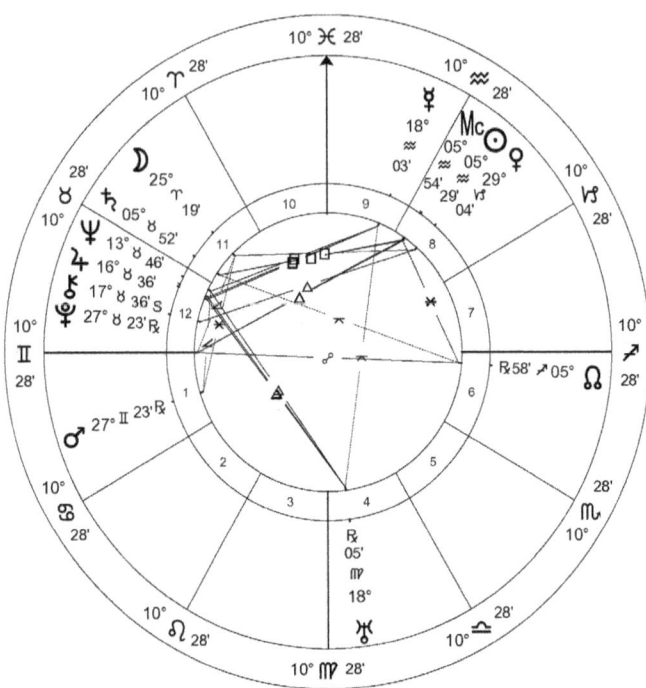

Chart 13: *Virginia Woolf; January 25, 1882, 12:15 PM; London, England*

alone, so we may have to integrate the aspect we consider important into the whole chart for a better chart picture. It's like zooming out to view a particular aspect, to see all the degrees around, but then to zoom it back, to integrate it into the whole life picture. So, if you zoom in regarding her Pluto-Venus aspect, you will see very important key factors of the chart.

At first glance, you can see the Stellium in the 12th house and the 8th house is emphasized (Sun conjunct both MC and Venus). Hence you can comprehend the intense activities behind the scenes, questions about life and death, that which we are allowed to see, and the risk of taking further, extra steps (her Sun is in the 8th house). In addition, her chart shows as dominant elements just earth and air, meaning a great predisposition to materialize her abstract thoughts, demonstrating, in a practical and efficient way, her detachment and her rational point of view. By contrast, her chart shows weak fire element and no planets in water signs. Her perception about emotions could have been abstract and very different than others and she could have perceived the world in a unique and detached way. Maybe this is the reason her style of writing was recognized, because it was different. Moreover, her life directions show optimism, confidentiality, enthusiasm, and shadow that could be reflected in her books (just the North Node and the Moon are in the Fire Element).

Pluto in Collaboration with Mars

This combination controls the speed of the energy that drives us in the world. Mars highlights impulses and actions, while Pluto controls the intentional plans. Mars represents the courage to act and to lead in a given situation, the desire to achieve something important in life. Pluto may symbolically treat Mars like a little brother, but these two brothers could generate dangerous manifestations and actions, if they are not controlled under parental principles.

Pluto is known as the higher octave of Mars; the little brother may have an ego, while the old brother may have power over him. Also, the little one may have anger and act in a spontaneous way, while the older one may have patience and could be determined to limit the effect of unhealthy energy. Mars is the soldier that may want war, to fight if he is upset, while Pluto acts behind the scenes; his actions are equally destructive in many cases. This is not a favorable combination. I have found this combination of Mars and Pluto in many criminals or victims' charts. It stimulates an obsessive passion, one that can lead a person to an inappropriate destination.

Nevertheless, Mars in connection with Pluto may have karmic issues or have some connection to crime, slavery, rape, brutality, torture or violence, violent death or murder. There may be an irresistible passion in that moment to act violently and to be determined to kill; hence the criminal might lack discernment in the moment of acting. In one of my cases, this aspect shows a violent death as the result of cruel revenge. However, Pluto in combination with Mars can also be benefic, especially if the person is motivated to do something positive with the excess energy.

Examples of Pluto in Collaboration with Mars

Kim Jong Un

Kim Jong Un is the Supreme leader of North Korea, the son of Kim Jong Il (1941–2011) and the grandson of Kim Il Sung (1912–1994). He has Pluto in Scorpio conjunct Mars in Libra. Also, the Pluto-Mars conjunction sextiles the Stellium formed by Jupiter-Neptune and Mercury. Theoretically, this Stellium might massively support Kim Jong's actions: Jupiter is associated with expansion, excess and exaggeration, and faith, while Neptune is associated with dreams, chaos and disintegration, confusion, fantasies, idealism, sacrifice, and even disillusion. On the other hand, Mercury shows mature thoughts, but he seems not to understand the informative world very well, or he may comprehend it in a very different way than most people.

The conjunction between Pluto and Mars is quite disturbing; however, Mars is influenced by Venus. So, his hidden actions seem to be in equilibrium, even though he shows cold thoughts, ideas, and plans he can act diplomatically. Furthermore, Mars is in a cardinal sign, which indicates that his ego could motivate his ambition to continue some of his actions that are already initiated. Moreover, Mars is the only planet in an air sign which shows us that through his activities, he might be connected to the innovating, civilized world. Additionally, he was born under the Crescent Moon Phase which may suggest that he wants to have momentum, to demonstrate his real identity in the world. Nevertheless, he could have a lot of imagination, fantasy and might be confused in terms of universal values.

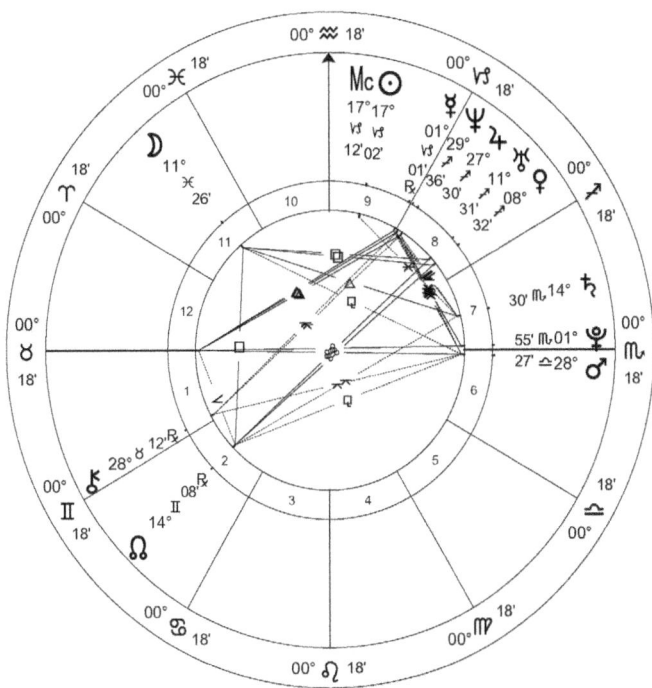

Chart 14: *Kim Jong Un; Jsanuary 8, 1984, time unknown; Pyongyang, North Korea*

Hugo Rafael Chávez Frías

Hugo Chavez was a Venezuelan politician who was president of Venezuela from 1999 until his death in 2013. If the time of birth is correct, he might have had tremendous inner motivations to initiate things in life. Also, he could have had a massive capacity to hold affection, to nurture others, and perhaps he could have been very popular in his country. He seems to have been born to be the center of attention. In his own platform of manifestation, many hidden plans could have been challenged his individuality. The Sun is in Leo and Pluto is in Leo, bringing it under the Sun's principles. Pluto in Leo (2nd) trines Mars

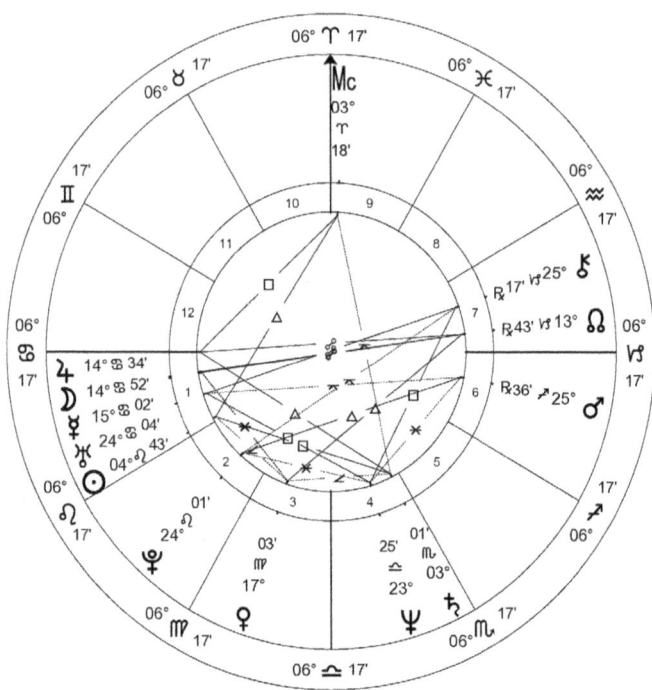

Chart 15: Hugo Chavez; July 28, 1954, 4:00 AM; Sabaneta, Venezuela

in Sagittarius (6th) and sextiles Neptune in Libra (4th). In this chart, the aspect between Pluto and Mars seems to be positive. Pluto is vitalized by the Sun, and Neptune in Libra acts as a mediator between the two, highlighting ideal negotiations skills. Neptune in the 4th house is the focal point of The Minor Grand Trine aspect pattern. Hence, his big dreams could have related to his natal country, and he could have sacrificed his individual dreams in favour of the more important ideals of his country.

Ioan Clamparu

Ioan Clamparu was accused of heading one of the biggest Romanian mafia groups, with dealings in human trafficking. He

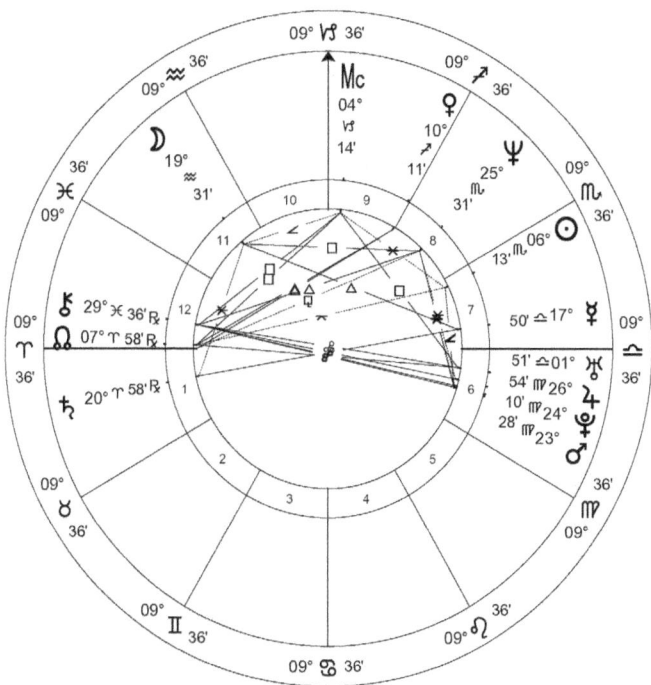

Chart 16: Ioan Clamparu; October 29, 1968, time unknown; Botosani, Romania

was arrested for the initiation and establishment of an international criminal organization and was sentenced to 30 years in prison by a court in Madrid. Even without knowing his time of birth, we can see Pluto conjunct Mars with an orb of one degree and Pluto is also conjunct Jupiter. He also has a Stellium in Virgo which automatically gives us details about how tactical and well organized he is in using his power.

Pluto in Collaboration with Jupiter

This will magnify power of all kinds, including wealth. However, in order to feel abundance, ask yourself: are you a generous spirit? Do you appreciate what you already have? Do you have a positive approach to life? How much knowledge are you ready to comprehend from the outside world? What do you know about other cultures, religions? Are you concerned with injustices? How is your belief system? Are you confident or wise enough? Imagine what someone can do with strong confidence and enormous power! They could create expansion in everything they do and create faith, a power that nobody can break or take from you. This is the type of wealth that each soul might want to have. This brings real happiness and compassion towards others. Jupiter sees the bigger picture and a wider framework.

I have Pluto in Libra (6th) square Jupiter conjunct Venus in Cancer (3rd). Also, Pluto works under Venus's principles, that is the ruler of my chart. However, theoretically, this is a major negative aspect that brought me a very delicate moment that challenged my belief system and human values. Pluto is about death, while Jupiter is about trust, belief, and faith. The 6th house is about health, everyday routine, while the 3rd house is about the early environment, grandparents. I was very young, around 13 years old, when my paternal grandmother had an accident, and she needed surgery, which was too difficult to perform because of other health issues. No one gave her any chances to live. I have watched my family members as they cried in disbelief. I remember seeing them losing faith and thinking to myself that she will make it.

I had discovered and developed a strong faith since I was nine years old, and this was a test for my belief system. I prayed for my grandmother, and I visited her every day; it was part of my routine after school; (3rd = school/ 6th = daily routines). I did not give up; I was not discouraged by doctors' opinions. Although I was the youngest member of the family, I became the most optimistic one. I fought in my mind with the demoralized idea that everyone else had about my grandmother's health. I was 100% convinced that she would live, and she did. Many of the neighbours who were troubled about her condition eventually died before her, as did my grandfather.

My grandmother lived more for than 12 years after that event. This is just one example of Pluto square Jupiter. There are so many different forms, layers, and variety of challenges that, if we understand, will give consistency to our character. A negative aspect often requires facing a significant challenge before something beautiful happens.

Traditionally, Jupiter is associated with benefits and luck, but in my view, Jupiter is more a form of reward, a personal achievement when you work with yourself. This can also inspire confidence. In addition, we attract benefits when we strongly believe. Pluto engaging with Jupiter might test our higher knowledge, morality, spiritual approach, kindness, and will refresh our belief system. Also, it can empower that individual or that country with a strong base of morality and generosity. At a negative level, this combination may expand the growth of international terrorism, and massive negative and dark actions. Moreover, some astrologers associate this planetary combination with an impact on economic cycles.

Examples of Pluto in Collaboration with Jupiter

Warren Edward Buffett

Warren Buffett is an American business magnate, investor, and philanthropist. He is considered one of the most successful investors in the world and has a net worth of US $82 billion as of July 18, 2019, making him the third-wealthiest person in the world.

He has Pluto conjunct Jupiter in Cancer in the 7th house. Also, this Pluto-Jupiter conjunction squares Venus is Libra (10th) and Uranus in Aries (4th). So, Pluto conjunct Jupiter is the focal point of a Cardinal Grand Trine which highlights opportunities to initiate and expand his wealth. He may have an inner powerful generosity for people in need.

Moreover, Pluto sesquiquadrates the Moon in Sagittarius (12th). Despite this, Jupiter is in mutual reception with the Moon

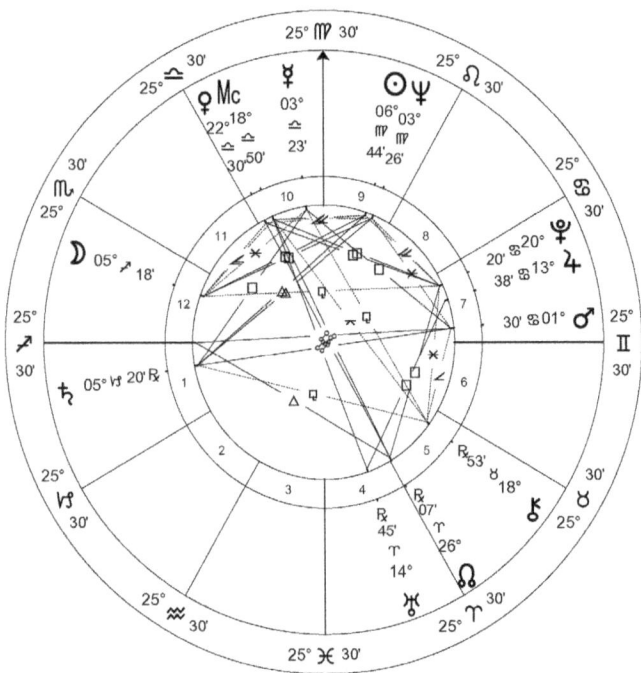

*Chart 17: Warren Buffett, August 30, 1930, 3:00 PM;
Omaha, Nebraska*

(12th), supporting each one of their principles. Consequently, his instinctive responses could have helped him to gain powerful trusted partnerships. Nevertheless, this Pluto-Jupiter conjunction seems to challenge his vocation while mediating the conflict between his values and his freedom, his money and his eccentricity (Venus conjunct MC and opposite Uranus).

Bill Gates

Bill Gates is an American tech millionaire, the richest man in the world in the nineties. He has Pluto conjunct Jupiter in Leo (2nd), the house of money and personal growth. This is a very important aspect because he has the Earth element missing

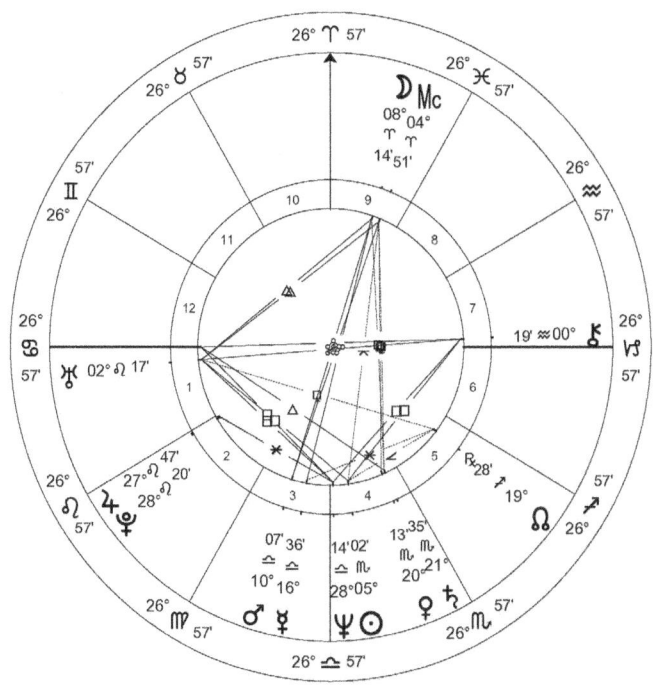

Chart 18: Bill Gates; October 28, 1955, 10:00 PM; Seattle, Washington

in his natal chart, an element that has to do with practicality and managing money. Apparently, he may have many challenges in terms of making money and perceiving reality in the way the majority do. However, Pluto (2nd) is in mutual reception with the Sun (4th). Furthermore, his plans could have been in synchronicity with his ideals, positively supported by his passion and obsession, his control over what he knows, and his ability to transform things that don't work (Sun conjunct Neptune, while Pluto sextile Neptune). Nevertheless, his needs in this existence seem to be connected to his vocation. He could have the feeling of new beginnings, independence, and take time to publicly express his opinions, his social dreams. (He was born under

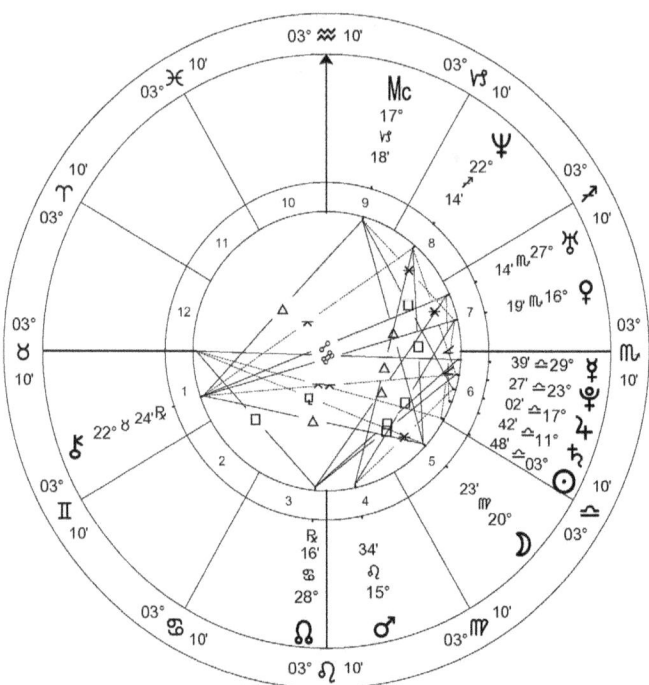

***Chart 19: Serena Williams: September 26, 1981, 8:28 PM;
Saginaw, Michigan***

the Gibbous Moon Phase, Moon conjunct MC (9th), also trine Uranus (1st).

Serena Williams

Serena Williams is an American professional tennis player, ranked by the Women's Tennis Association (WTA) as No. 1 in the world in singles on eight occasions. She has Pluto conjunct Jupiter and Mercury in Libra in the 6th house. She is Libran with a Taurus Ascendant. Therefore, Venus has double significance, being the dispositor of her Sun and her Ascendant. However, Venus is in Scorpio (7th), so her characteristics in terms of others, partnering, and relationships are symbolically under

Plutonian energy. Venus is in mutual reception to Pluto. In this case, Pluto doesn't work alone; Jupiter's energy and that of Mercury stimulates Pluto. As you can see, Pluto conjunct Jupiter emphasizes her daily work (6th), magnifying her professional results, and transforming her ideas of trust and values.

Pluto in Collaboration with Saturn

Worldwide, this conjunction creates history. Each time, when this aspect comes to a culmination point, something important happens in the world. At a globallevel, Pluto conjunct Saturn appeared during the First World War (1914), as well as during the economy stagnation of 1982. Starting with late September 1914, Pluto was conjunct Saturn in the second degree of Cancer. History shows that the First Battle of the Marne was fought to the north and east of Paris in early September 1914.

This aspect of energy could come in intense waves, a longtime dispute between two powers that are usually friendly. One of the powers could act strategically, in a disciplined way; the other may be the hidden one, having secret plans to act. So, this combination might bring power issues and fears of losing power, especially if the power was used in an abusive way. However, Pluto wants to eliminate the feeling of guilt, the abusive dictatorial power to investigate the structure of that organization or society. We as humans admire and see just the final page of a person, their great achievements, but we don't see the real suffering, the hard work behind each step. Saturn may work well: organized, systematic, having self-control, and patience under Pluto's influences. Consequently, the results could have a superior form. In contrast, this aspect may bring self-destruction, a failed regeneration of the way someone organizes their life.

Examples of Pluto in Collaboration with Saturn

Liz Greene

Liz Greene is an American-British astrologer and author,

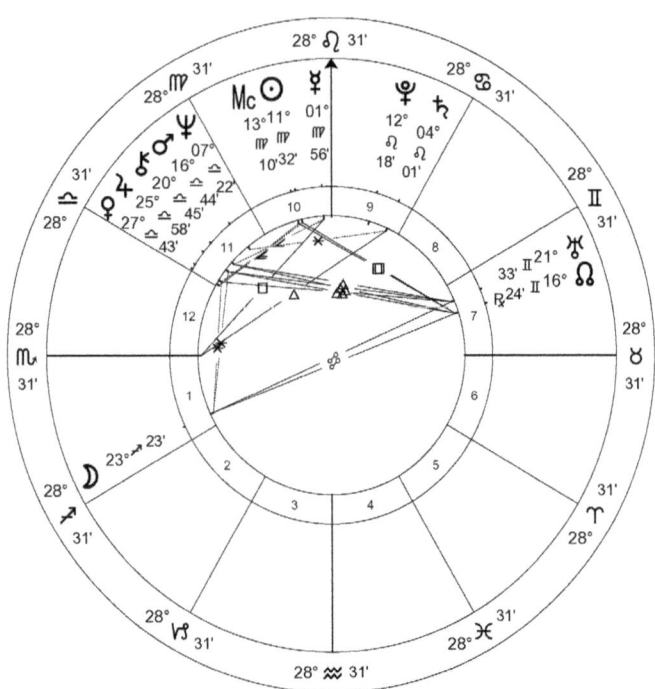

Chart 20: Liz Greene; September 4, 1946, 1:01 PM; Englewood, New Jersey

Jungian analyst and lecturer and one of the most highly respected astrologers of the 20th century. She has a Scorpio Ascendant; hence Pluto is the ruler of her chart. Pluto is conjunct Saturn in Leo, in the 9th house of publications, higher education and research. The ruler of this conjunction is the Sun, which is conjunct MC in Virgo in the 10th. Hence, the chart shows a public figure who has superiority and power to express her philosophical view worldwide and to dominate or even control her field.

Edward Snowden

Edward Snowdon is a former American technical contractor and a Central Intelligence Agency (CIA) employee, who

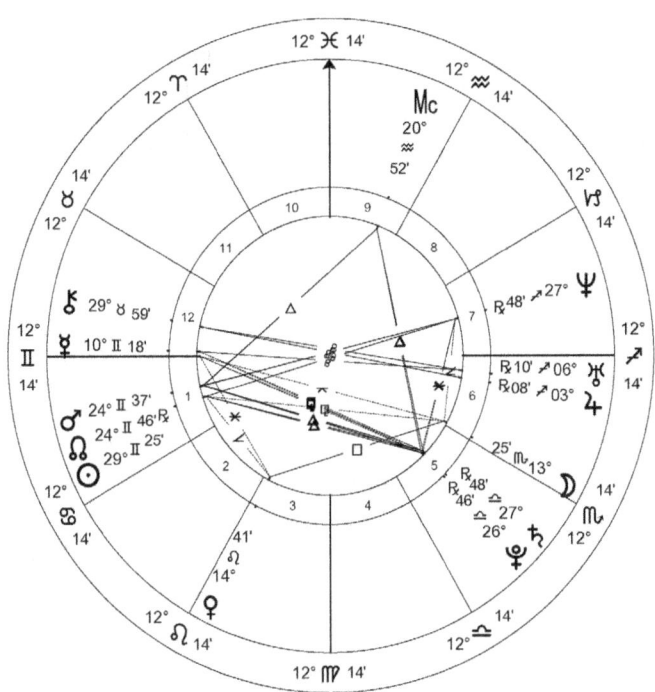

Chart 21: Edward Snowdon; June 21, 1983, 4:42 AM; Elizabeth City, North Carolina

disclosed details of a classified NSA spy program to the press. He is a Gemini with a Gemini Ascendant. Moreover, Mercury, the dispositor of his Sun, and his Ascendant is a rising planet, too, being conjunct the ASC. So, Mercury has triple importance in this chart. Furthermore, Mercury is sesquiquadrate (135°) Pluto, which might bring stressful situations in terms of information and communication. He also has Pluto conjunct Saturn in Libra in the 5th house, both trine Mars, the Sun and North Node in Gemini (1st). Additionally, this set of aspects represent the base that positively supports his life vocation. Pluto is part of a Grand Trine in Air.

Nevertheless, Pluto conjunct Saturn in the 5th may stimulate his passion to research and investigate the things that were under his control and caused him to act like a mediator, as the conjunction is in a cardinal sign, Libra. Also, Pluto is part of The Minor Grand Trine that may show an extra opportunity for him to realize a big dream in regard to others, while sacrificing his personal dream. Pluto sextiles Neptune in Sagittarius (7th). In other words, Pluto is part of a complex configuration, a pattern aspect called *The Kite*.

Steven Spielberg,

Steven Spielberg is an American film producer and director, and the winner of an Academy Award for Best Director. He is considered to be one of the founding pioneers of the New Hollywood era and one of the most popular directors and producers in film history.

First of all, Scorpio, the sign of Pluto, dominates the chart. He was also born under a Scorpio Moon, Third Quarter of Lunar Phase, which highlights his profound need to act based of his wisdom and to have a deep connection to his public. Pluto conjuncts Saturn in Leo, is sextile Neptune and square Jupiter, Venus and the Moon. As you can see Pluto is part of the Minor Grand Trine, where Neptune is the focal point. Additionally, his chart shows no personal or social planets in the Air element, just Neptune and Uranus. Hence, Neptune, representing the movies, a form of high expression and a universal gift, seems to be the channel that connects him to the abstract world. Nevertheless, his big ideals seem well supported by the conjunction of Pluto and Saturn.

On the other hand, the Jupiter/Venus conjunction (in Pluto's sign, Scorpio) shows a higher form of generosity and compassion, and being in the 5th house it's notsurprising that he has several adopted kids. I associate adoption with Scorpio or Pluto, which represent a form of total change, a regeneration of someone's life. Additionally, with Pluto conjunct Saturn in Leo, according to *Astrodatabank* 'Spielberg became a Knight of the British Empire, one of the highest honours bestowed by Queen Elizabeth II and

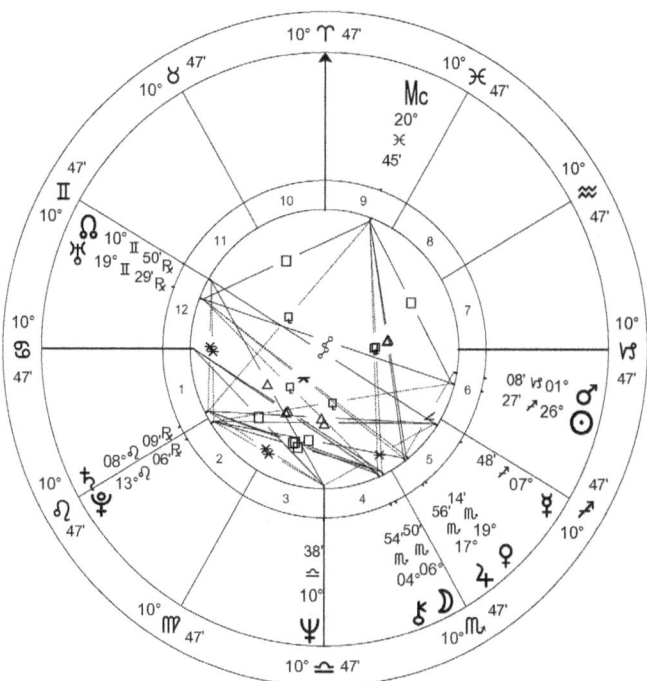

Chart 22: Steven Spielberg; December 18, 1946, 6:16 PM; Cincinnati, Ohio

a special tribute for an American, on 1/29/2001, Washington, DC.'

Pluto in Collaboration with Chiron

I have heard this expression that I immediately associated with Chiron: 'guilt is to the spirit what pain is to the body.' Pluto, in collaboration with Chiron, will want to burn every corner and angle of suffering, the shadow of any wounds, and then it may empower the spirit to heal the rest of the body. Pluto will carefully investigate the body and mind of someone to eliminate those things that could weaken us, even situations that could bring physical pain. The moment of confrontation could feel uncomfortable, but once it is acknowledged it can be perma-

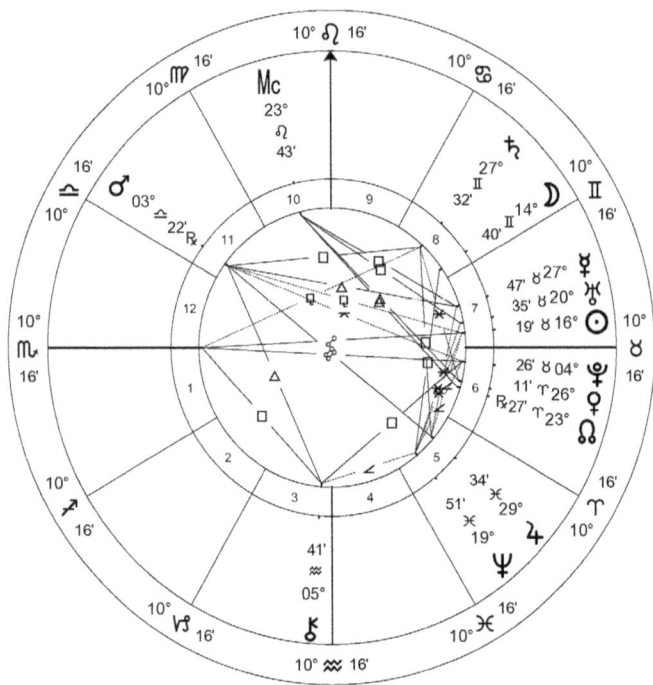

Chart 23: Sigmund Freud; May 6, 1856, 6:30 PM; Freiberg/ Mahren, Czech Republic

nently removed.

Examples of Pluto in Collaboration with Chiron

Sigmund Freud

Sigmund Freud was an Austrian neurologist and the founder of psychoanalysis, a clinical method for treating psychopathology through dialogue between a patient and a psychoanalyst. Freud has Pluto in Taurus (6th) square Chiron in Aquarius (3rd). This aspect may briefly describe the type of job Freud did, how he did it, and why.

Chiron represents the body and spirit, and in my view, under the influence of Chiron we can symbolically connect our body and spirit. Chiron is in Aquarius in the 3rd, the house of communication, face-to face dialog, and healing through dialog (something rare). On the other hand, Freud has his Ascendant in Scorpio which emphasizes the importance of Pluto. Furthermore, Pluto is in Taurus, conjunct the Descendant from the 6th house, which highlights his intense work with the goal to stabilize things and to give power and security to others, with the purpose of redefining them.

E.H. Troinski

E.H. Troinski was a German professional astrologer best known for his advocacy of Tertiary directions, a data collector. He dedicated a large part of his astrological career to the area of mundane astrology. He has Pluto in Gemini (10th) conjunct the MC. Also, Pluto trines Chiron in Aquarius (6th) and sextiles Saturn in Aries (8th). As you can see, Pluto is part of the Minor Grand Trine. Despite these positive aspects of Pluto, his natal chart also shows Pluto opposite both the Sun in Sagittarius and Venus in Capricorn (4th). The energy that was generated and transformed by his inner power could have had roots in many different life zones. However, I have chosen to use the example of Pluto trine Chiron in Aquarius (6th). He may not have had a persuasive career (Pluto in the 10th) without daily work, or an intense passion in that direction. His Chiron in Aquarius (6th) could have shaped his spirit, helping him understand the power behind his soul. His daily routine seems to support his career, his slow way of manifesting things in the world. He seems to have had that connection to the Universe in a unique/rebellious way.

We know that he was an eccentric among German astrologers and created some interesting theories beyond the bounds of traditional astrology. I associate Chiron with astrology, and with Aquarius, the sign that can be perceived as an abstract original platform for the manifestation of the spirit.

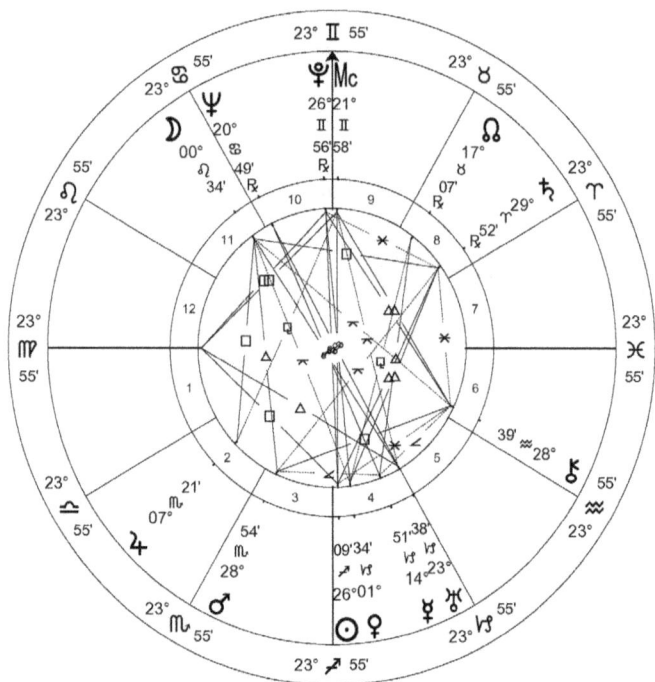

Chart 24: E.H. Troinski; December 18, 1910, 11:45 PM; Berlin, Germany

Pluto in Collaboration with Uranus

Like Pluto, Uranus is an outer planet and its influences could affect a specific area of our life for years. We know that Uranus brings unexpected changes that could be essential to prevent stagnation in someone's life, while Pluto might secretly want us to explore and play with our inner potential. In other words, we could hide our eccentric impulse while our passion creates a secret platform to manifest our originality.

Pluto engaging with Uranus may bring about a powerful eruption, after a long time of feeling powerless. It may redefine our incarnation in an abstract way. So, it could trigger our hidden rebels and might open an avenue to extend the individual human capacity, which can later be applied to a group. As we know, people are tempted to make radical decisions during life crises, even if it is about a change of hairstyle relocating, or quitting a job. At a universal level, it may bring radical reform, a disruption of everything and everyone who holds social power abusively. The dynamics of these two planets are so intense and develop over such a long period of time, that for us, as a generation, it is impossible not to feel it.

Examples of Pluto in Collaboration with Uranus

Jeffrey Preston Bezos

Jeff Bezos is an American technology entrepreneur and investor. He is thefounder, CEO, and president of Amazon.com. Briefly, he has Pluto conjunct Uranus in Virgo, one of the most analytical, methodical, and practical signs. We know that Amazon is a powerful business which caused many small businesses to close, as Amazon keeps expanding and dominating the online market. Also, Uranus trines Mercury in Capricorn which highlights the practicality, efficiency and convenience of ecommerce; Mercury is the dispositor of this Pluto-Uranus conjunction.

Bashar al-Assad

Bashar al Assad has been President of Syria since July 17, 2000. He is commander-in-chief of the Syrian Armed Forces and Regional Secretary of the Arab Socialist branch in Syria. Even though we don't know his time of birth, his natal chart shows that Pluto is part of an Earth Stellium. Pluto is conjunct both Uranus and the Sun in Virgo and opposite Saturn and the Moon in Pisces. Hence, the chart might suggest major contradictions between his powerful, rebel individuality and the complex set of world rules and his needs. Furthermore, he might like to study, to research social truth and religions, analyzing the

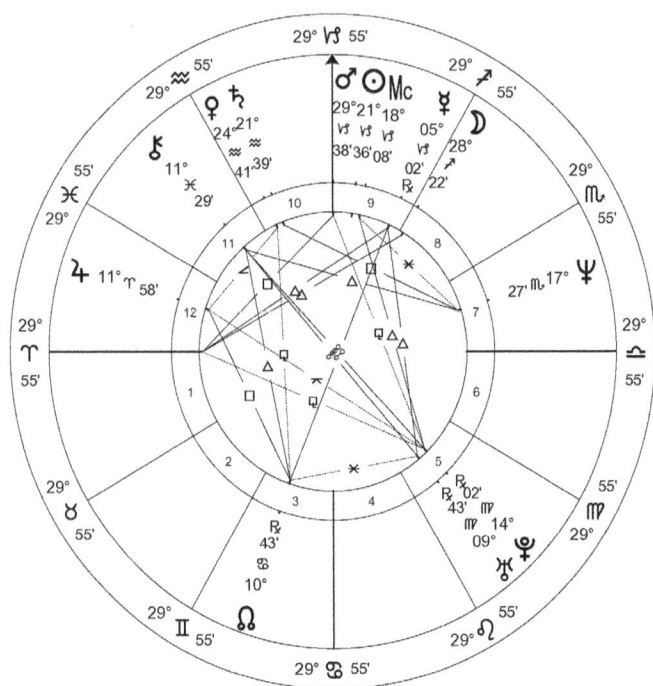

Chart 25: Jeff Bezos; January 12, 1964, 12:00 PM; Albuquerque, New Mexico

things that are behind the science. Moreover, his needs are in some way philanthropist, towards people, while he might not like to involve emotions in his daily routines. Consequently, he may experience emotional difficulties, unusual breaks, and unpredictable actions. Additionally, he might not comprehend the sense of authority like most people. He could act in a unique, unusual way when he feels confident, and must initiate actions.

Momcilo Luburic

Doctor Luburic is a Professor of Law, author, and the Founder of the "Dimitrie Cantemir" Christian University, that received the High Degree Trust, the highest distinction awarded

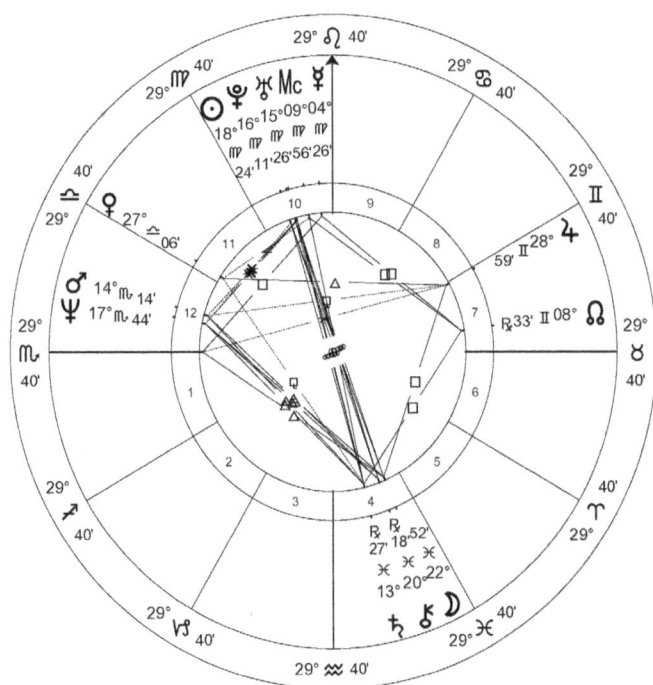

Chart 26: *Bashar al Assad; September 11, 1965, time unknown; Damascus, Syria*

to a higher education institution in Romania.

Although he was born in another country (Serbia), after receiving his PhD in law (Romania), he has chosen to live and teach law in Romania at the Faculty of Law, Bucharest. Furthermore, after the communist regime ended, he had an inner determination, power, and eccentric view to introduce a new form of higher education in Romania: a private University, with high standards, and with new locations in many cities in Romania. At that time, private education did not exist in Romania, and it was not easy to implement. The process of obtaining all the accreditations and permits was long and intense. He was in a long legal battle with the Minister of Education in Romania. On top of this, he had to deal with people's mentality at that time,

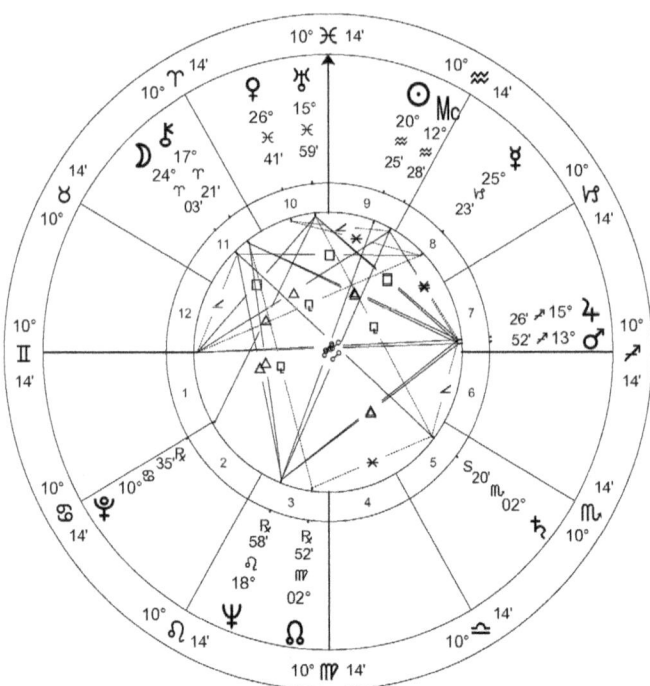

Chart 27: Momcilo Luburic: February 10, 1924, time unknown; Bilec, Yugoslavia

because the majority were not open to this new type of institution in their country. He has reinvented the old form of higher education, redefined it a complex form (Uranus is in Pisces), expanding the possibilities for students not only to have the best facilities, the top teachers but also to have access and to practice in an important government institutions during their studies.

He has Pluto trine Uranus, a major positive aspect that supports his high ideals and social vocation. He has a conservative mind and at the same time, an innovative social view. Uranus is vital in his chart because it is the dispositor of his Sun. Uranus is associated with the higher mind, while Pluto, redefined and reborn, represents the regenerating force, wisdom born out of difficulty.

Momcilo Luburic was my teacher and my mentor for about four years, and also a close soul. However, only after I relocated to Chicago, he told me that his father once lived in Chicago, too, and fought in the Serbia revolution. At that time, his family was separated. His Saturn, representing the father figure is in Scorpio, Pluto's sign.

Pluto in Collaboration with Neptune

Under Neptune and Pluto influences, we might have a deep passion to find a way towards perfection. What could happen when we don't find fulfilment? We may be tempted to escape, to sacrifice our reality, to lose control, slowly destroying our big ideals. Then, chaos and disintegration may appear. It could be the first step before our total transformation.

We can think of so many homeless people who may have lost track of life, because of their vulnerability, trust in others, sensibility, and because others might not trust their imagination, powerful creativity or supreme gifts. If some of the richest souls die prematurely, society could lose a treasure, an essential step towards progress and evolution. We can think what would have happened if well-known inventors had been in a situation where they interrupted their life ideals; major delays or lack of progress would likely exist in technology and the evolution of humankind in general. So, next time you pass by a lost soul, think about the possibility: what if that person is gifted but never had the chance or the inner force to perfect developing their goal.

The world is a big casting process, and the people are the actors of the world. The role you may have is the talent that supports you during your existence. The talent might need to be built, sometimes in secret, to escape the ordinary and stay on the imaginary platform. Who wins is who has an inner force to survive and then to control their destiny. Through Neptune's window, some of us can visualize the Universe as an infinite art.

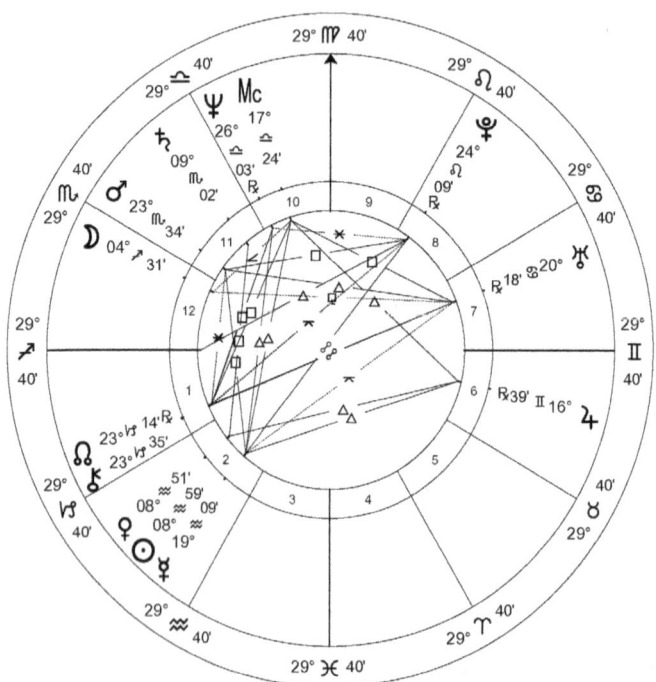

Chart 28: Oprah Winfrey; January 29, 1954, 4:30 AM; Kosciusko, Mississippi

It may be like walking through a zone of unreality. Neptune allows our vision to reach just that point where we are individually prepared to see it. That is why a rich art never dies, because its meaning is always interpreted differently by a highly attuned soul.

On the other hand, Pluto, the 'lord of the darkness,' will protect your soul in the most intense life moments, and eventually will fight with death. This power only works in secret; darkness, not light, is necessary to see its power. It will nurture your soul, and it may make a pact with it; its power may break through boundaries, and wisdom could be re-born from difficulties. Your imagination is rich and powerful, even if others do not perceive it. And your gift must be supported and grow with passion.

Examples of Pluto in Collaboration with Neptune

Oprah Winfrey

Oprah Winfrey is an American talk-show hostess, actress and business executive. Born illegitimate and virtually abandoned in the Deep South, she is a living symbol of the self-made person in spite of all odds. She is one of the best known and highest paid entertainers of the '90s with her TV talk show and business ventures.

She has Pluto in Leo (8th) sextile Neptune in Libra (10th). Pluto empowers her big ideals and vitalizes her force in terms of public expression. Pluto doesn't support just her high ideals; it helps her natural talent of putting her wisdom into action. (She was born under the Third Quarter Phase Moon) supporting her big dreams. Pluto indirectly activates her healing force; so, she can easily follow her path in helping others, despite some inhibitions (Pluto quincunx Chiron and North Node in Capricorn.) Chiron is the only body in the Earth element, so receiving input from Pluto could influence how she sees the real world. Moreover, her chart shows many crises in terms of her actions, obstacles that could decrease her enthusiastic energy (Pluto square Mars in Scorpio). Actually, Pluto is part of a Fire Grand Trine that could allow her to reinvent her individuality and her humanitarian approach. Moreover, Pluto trine Ascendant in the last degree of Sagittarius highlights her powers in terms of new beginnings

Quentin Tarantino

Other examples could be Quentin Tarantino, an American filmmaker, actor, film programmer, and cinema owner. His films are characterized by nonlinear storylines, satirical subject matter and aestheticization of violence. He has Pluto in Virgo sextile

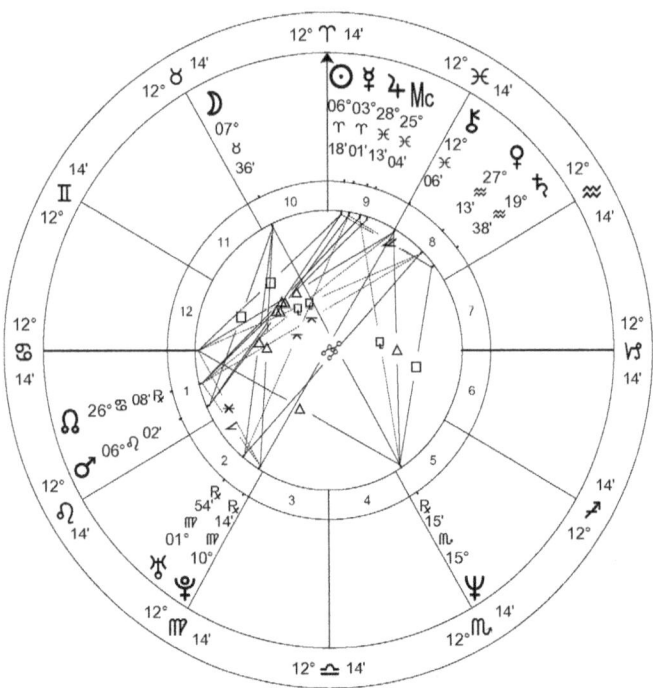

Chart 29: Quentin Tarantino; March 27, 1963, 12:00 PM; Knoxville, Tennessee

Neptune in Scorpio, Pluto's sign. Neptune is the planet associated with film and industries associated with the arts; being in Scorpio reflects the type of movie he makes. Furthermore, Mars, Pluto's little brother, is in mutual reception with the Sun.

Secondary Influences

Pluto in contact with the ASC may describe the type and power that supports our beginnings. It might influence how to observe and comprehend things in life. Hence, the power of beginnings might contour the individual character during this incarnation and will stimulate passion towards everything associated with Pluto: investigation, secret actions,

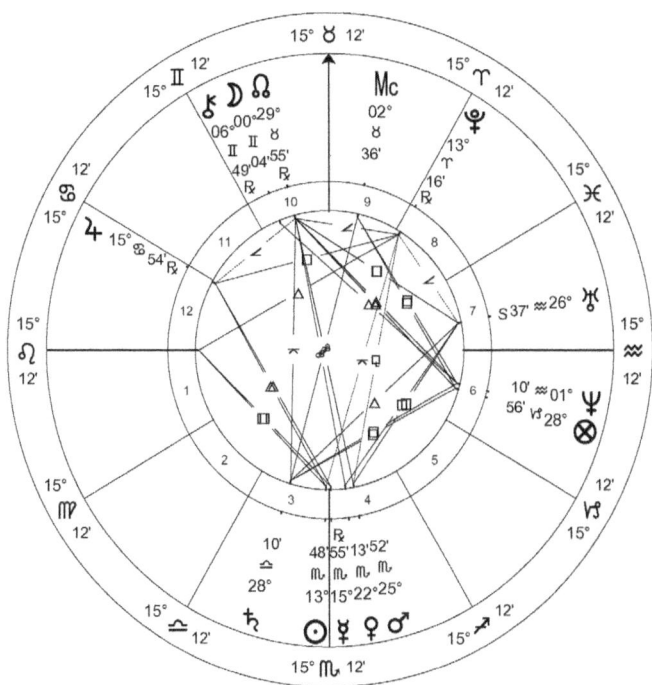

Chart 30: Cesare Lombroso; November 6, 1835, 11:00 PM; Verona Italy

control of power, etc.

Chart Examples:

Cesare Lomboso

A very good example is this case is Cesare Lombroso, The Father of Criminology; Italian criminologist, physician, and founder of the Italian School of Positivist Criminology. Lombroso's theory of anthropological criminology essentially stated that criminality was inherited and that someone "born criminal" could be identified by physical defects, skulls, and facial features.

In his chart, Pluto trine Ascendant shows his approach to

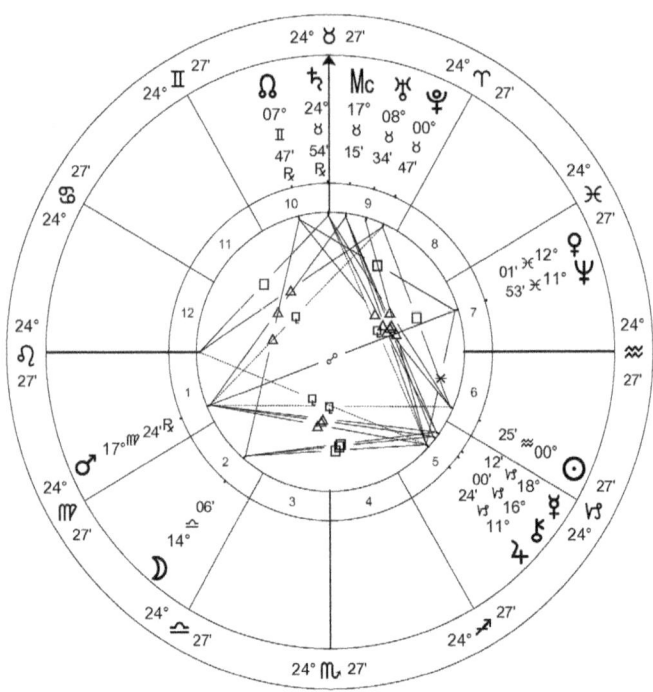

Chart 31: Eusapia Paladino; January 20, 1854, 7:00 PM; Minervino, Italy

life, looking for and researching evidence that could identify criminals. In addition, Scorpio is emphasized in his chart, having a Stellium in Scorpio (Sun, Mercury, Venus, and Mars are in Scorpio). Moreover, Pluto not only controls the power of those planets, but influences them. Furthermore, Pluto squares Jupiter in Cancer, the sign of initiation and security. So, his active passion for investigating, security protection, crimes and death could have brought a challenge to his belief system, his higher knowledge. Nevertheless, he did not have any planets in the earth element and no traditional planets in in the Fire element, with Pluto being the only planet in Fire.

Additionally, later in his life, Lombroso began investigat-

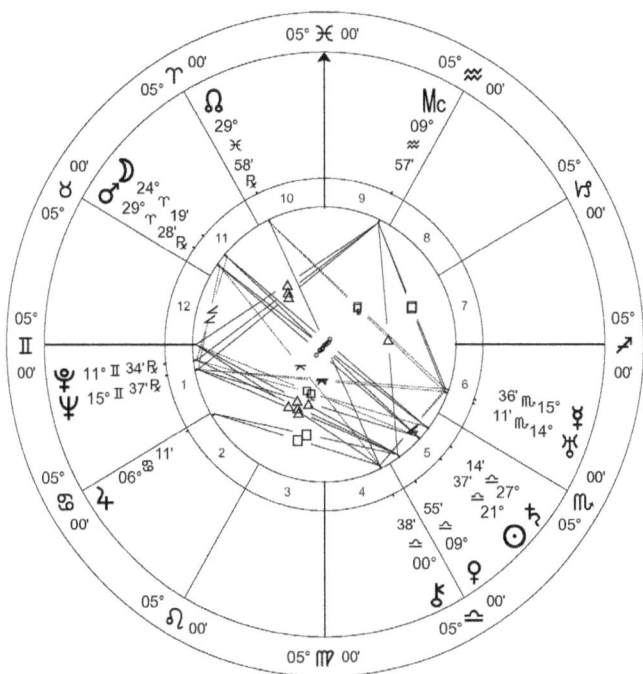

*Chart 32: E.E. Cummings; October 14, 1894, 7:00 PM;
Cambridge, Massachusetts*

ing mediumship. Lombroso discusses his views on the paranormal and spiritualism in his book *After Death – What?* (1909), in which he talks about his belief in the existence of spirits and claimed that the medium Eusapia Palladino was genuine. Therefore, you can recognize the strong influence of Pluto, which has shaped his way of seeing and navigating through life.

Eusapia Palladino

Eusapia Palladino was a 19th century Italian medium, the first physical medium who stood in the crossfire of worldwide collective investigation for more than 20 years. Her chart shows Pluto in Taurus (9th) trine ASC in Leo. Also, Pluto squares the

Sun in Aquarius (6th). Her Ascendant is very important because it is the only door that might have accessed the qualities of the fire element. Nevertheless, all the influences that the ascendant had received (including Pluto) could have helped her to build her confidentiality and enthusiasm.

E.E. Cummings

E.E. Cummings was an American poet, writer, painter, essayist, author, and playwright. He was one of the most popular poets of the 20th century; his verses have inspired countless readers. His Pluto is conjunct ASC and Neptune in Gemini. This combination defines his personality, highlights his intellect, his capacity, power, the imagination behind his thoughts and his inner force that transformed his everyday feelings.

Pluto is in a mutual reception to Mercury, which is the ruler of the chart (6th), highlighting his passion towards writing. Additionally, Pluto trine Venus in Libra, 5th, and MC in Aquarius, 9th. Therefore, Pluto describes his inner force, gives values to his self-expression, and has supported him in achieving his life vocation.

Pluto in Collaboration with the MC

We know that Pluto is an outer planet; being associated with a group, the house location of the MC is usually a public area, a non-familiar zone. So, practically, even if a person controls this energy, it may not be totally implemented to his own benefit.

The location of Pluto around the MC in the natal chart may influence the zone of public interest. In this public zone, there is passion, determination, secret work, and deep research to find a specific *treasure* that is up there in the world, in society. However, in a profound sense, for those having Pluto conjunct the MC in their chart that treasure belongs to them. These people may not feel the life regeneration if they do not achieve the deepest purpose of their soul. With the MC in the public zone, the per-

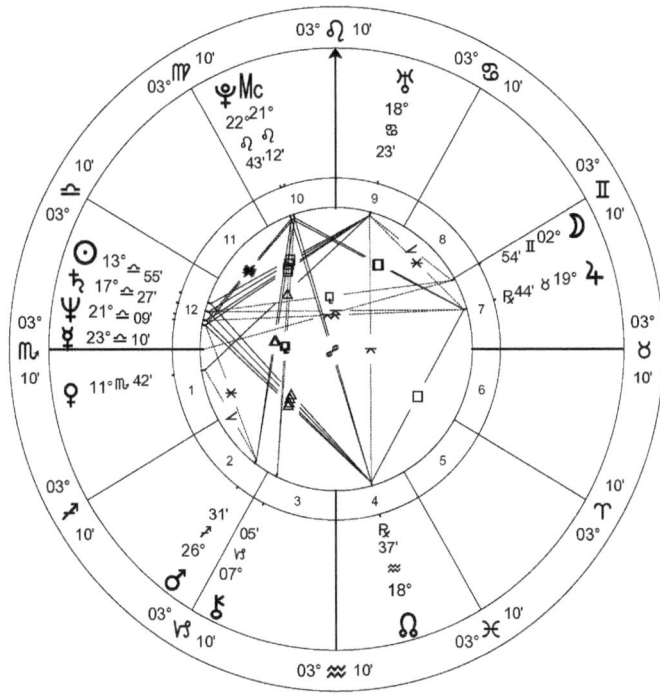

Chart 33: Vladimir Putin; October 7, 1952, 9:30 AM, St.Petersburg, Russia

sonal decisions of these people might affect others involuntarily.

On the other hand, even if Pluto in transit travels slowly towards the zone of others, like the 11th and 12th houses, the things that are collected from the surrounding areas will be brought back to the central station, to fill the soul vocation. Perhaps the most valuable transformation of Pluto is that he teaches us how to investigate each degree which it passes throughout life. If you learn its meaning along the way, you are already patient. With patience, we can have the clarity to discover any hidden layer of any career.

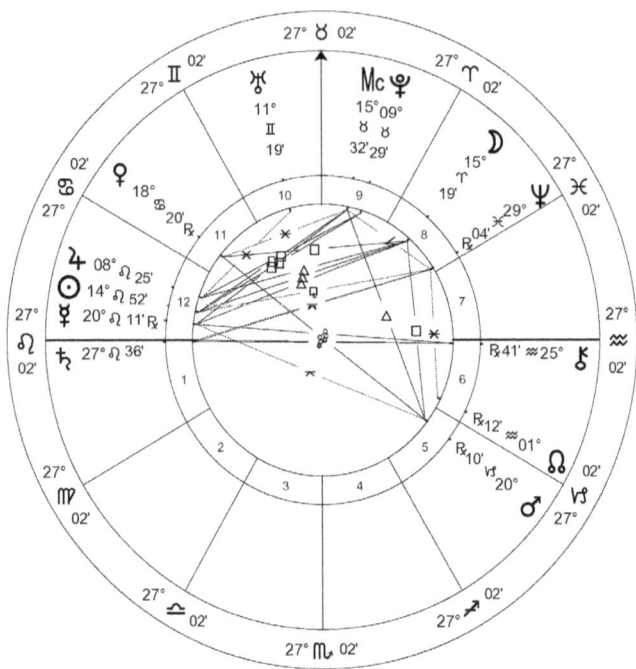

Chart 34: William Frederick Allan; August 7, 1860, 5:49 AM; Westminster, England

Chart Examples:

Vladimir Putin

Vladimir Putin is the President of Russia. He has Pluto conjunct the MC in Leo (10th). However, his chart shows a Scorpio Ascendant, so Pluto is the ruler of the chart. Furthermore, his Pluto sextiles Neptune and Mercury in Libra (12th). Moreover, Pluto squares Jupiter in Taurus (7th) and trines Mars in Sagittarius (2nd). Pluto activates his Stellium in the 12th house, where the Sun, Saturn, Mercury and Neptune are in conjunction. The dispositor of the Stellium is Venus, which is influenced by Pluto, being in Scorpio. Consequently, he could be very authoritarian and strict in terms of his role in life and public view; neverthe-

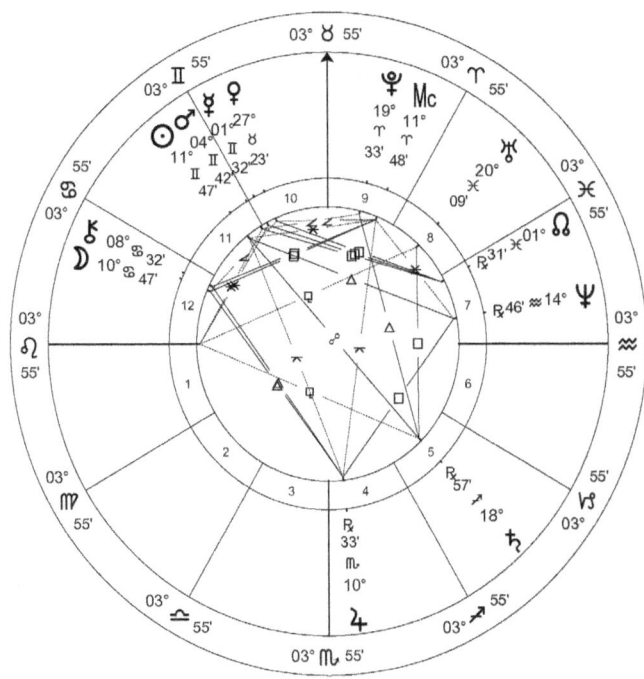

Chart 35: Thomas Hardy; June 2, 1840, 8:00 AM; Dorset, England

less having stable values to follow starting with the beginning of each plan.

Moreover, Pluto is part of The Minor Grand Trine, highlighting the natural power to diplomatically handle and control many areas of the world. His chart shows abilities to initiate what he already has started. As you can see, the energy of Pluto defines his vocation and his way of worldwide manifestation.

William Frederick Allan

William Frederick Allan, known as "Alan Leo" was a British astrologer, businessman and author, a Theosophist who is considered the father of modern astrology. His chart shows Pluto conjunct the MC in Taurus (9th), the house of publications, research and higher knowledge. Also, he is a Leo, with a Leo Ascendant; hence the Sun has double signification in this chart. However, Pluto squares the Sun in Leo (12th) which is conjunct both Jupiter and Mercury.

Symbolically, Pluto could have disturbed his creative individuality and his philosophical way of seeing the world. He could have had many challenges that could have revitalized his sense of destiny, and perhaps moved his higher knowledge back and forth. However, the chart shows that he has had a very confident base and detached way of seeing the world. Nevertheless, the challenges that he may have faced might have caused his inner force to materialize and fulfil his life purpose.

Thomas Hardy

Thomas Hardy was an architect and writer, a distinguished poet, and one of England's greatest late Victorian novelists. Hardy shattered Victorian values of the period in his brooding novels about change and death, and loss and decay set in the landscape of Dorset, England.

He has Pluto conjunct the MC in Aries (9th), highlighting the zone of publication and writing to fulfil his deep life purpose. Also, the chart shows that his Pluto trines Saturn in Sagittarius (5th), which allowed his passion to navigate freely, having philosophical self-expression. On the other hand, Sagittarius is the sign of Jupiter, and Jupiter is in Scorpio, coordinated by Pluto. Moreover, Pluto is in Mars' sign and semi-square Mars, part of a Gemini Stellium. Gemini is the sign of writing. It seems like he surrounded himself with intellectual, skilled people who may have inspired him to initiate ways of achieving his life's goals.

Pluto as Part of a Pattern Aspect

Nothing can be done perfectly without inner passion. There are so many personalities, especially people in power, excellent

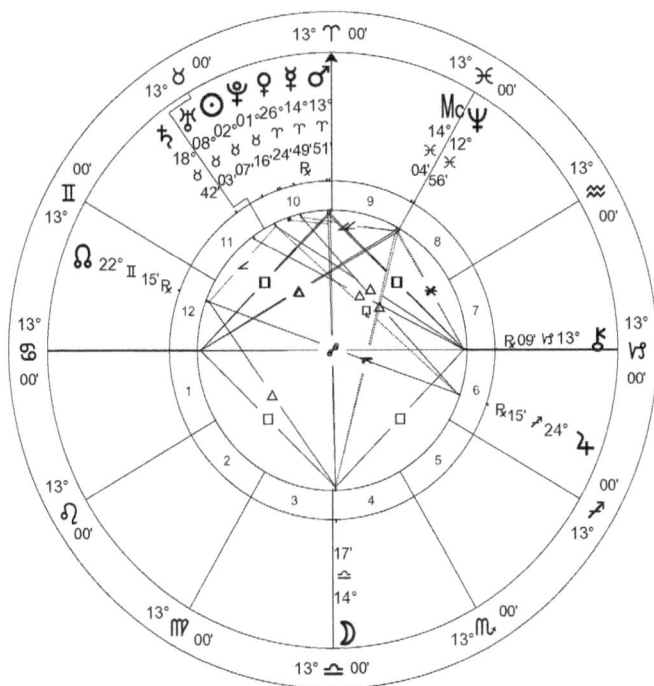

Chart 36: Alphonse Bertillon; April 22, 1853, 9:00 AM; Paris, France

surgeons, and people that redefine a specific field who have Pluto involved in one or more Pattern Aspects. However, I chose to share just three relevant examples of Pluto as a hidden power that can investigate things and regenerate human energy, empower and redefine someone.

Alphonse Bertillon

Alphonse Bertillion was a French police officer and biometrics research; created a mugshot identification system for criminals prior to the invention of fingerprinting. His Pluto is in Taurus (10th) conjunct the Sun in Taurus, with Uranus in Taurus and Venus in Aries. As you can see, Pluto is part of a Stellium which emphasized his passion and his determination to initiate

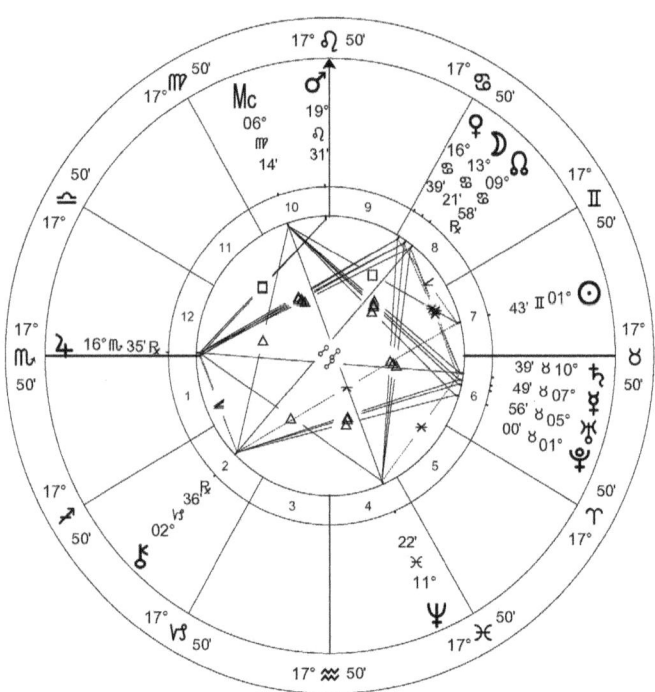

Chart 37: Hermann Kummell; May 22, 1852, 6:30 PM; Korrbach, Germany

powerful tools that brought some improvement to his field.

Hermann Kummell

Hermann Kummell was a German surgeon whose work involved the treatment of fractures, bone implants and diseases of the spinal column. He also conducted extensive research of bladder and kidney disturbances, diseases of the chest, etc. He was among the first surgeons to advocate removal of the appendix in cases of recurrent appendicitis, and in 1886 attempted the first choledochotomy.

He is a Gemini with a Scorpio Ascendant. Pluto, the ruler

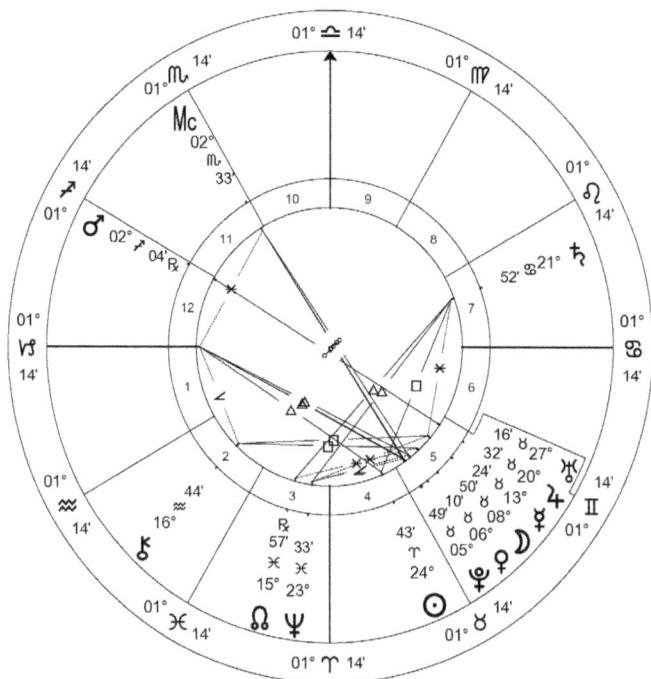

Chart 38: Emile Durkheim; April 15, 1858, 00:30 AM; Epinal, France

of his chart, conjuncts Uranus and Mercury (the dispositor of his Sun) in Taurus (6th). As you can see, Pluto is part of a fixed Stellium that emphasizes the 6th house (everyday routine, work, health). He has brought innovating ideas to his work. Consequently, he has been able to perform health transformations for others, and, to reinvent new medical methods of work. Additionally, the ruler of his chart, Pluto trines Chiron in Capricorn, (2nd) and the MC in Virgo (10th). Chiron represents medicine and healing, while Virgo (the sign of his MC) is associated with meticulous details and serving others.

Émile Durkheim

Emile Durkheim a French sociologist often called the father of sociology. His work helped lay the foundation for academia's acceptance of anthropology and sociology as sciences.

He has six planets in Taurus, 5th house: Pluto, Venus, Moon, Mercury, Jupiter and Uranus, emphasizing the zone of his self-expression. Pluto is part of Stellium being conjunct Venus and Moon that amplified the importance of powerful relationships and emotional stability. Actually, this mixed energy tells as all about his needs, his habits, dreams. So, his personal needs were connected to social groups and human values. Moreover, his MC is in Scorpio, Pluto's sign highlighting what type of platform required his life vocation. Despite the many contradictions between his various activities, free time and public manifestations; he has demonstrated passion towards social interaction, relationships, empirical investigation and critical analysis to develop a frame of knowledge about social order, acceptance, and social evolution. Consequently, he published The Rules of Sociological Method and set up the first European department of sociology, becoming France's first professor of sociology.

Reference

[1] A quote from Joyce Carol Oates.

The source of the data used in the example charts is astro.com and Wikipedia.

CHAPTER THREE

Pluto Transits the Natal Chart

"No age and no generation have been free of darkness."
                                Steven Forrest, The Book of Pluto

I will add to this: no person from our world is free of Pluto's influences. There are not magic umbrellas that may protect us from the world's "precipitation." The inner pressure and the burning process will exist for each of us, no matter how wealthy or influent we may be. The zones of your life that Pluto transits over time could be put under the magnifying glass of a world investigation. At an individual level, it's about how we are around others, even if the people around us over time shaped our personality in one way or another. Metaphorically, others will take layer by layer from your body for you to look into your soul despite any feelings of crudity.

However, we will likely have enough time to move to the zone we like, to the group we belong, to discover life the way we want. Also, we will have many avenues to explore and understand the world. However, all of our activities, life implications, and even our life results might be evaluated in such a profound way of self -purification. Secretly, the outside environment seems to scan us to revaluate our inner force, our human vibrations. Perhaps, our internal power moves us physically in the appropriated place for a human transformation. There seems to be a well-defined purpose for concealing any treasure. Consequently, there may be a day, a point in our life, when everything we worked for, will mean nothing because another source might open for us another life perspective to redefine the meaning of existence. Each of us has this opportunity to regenerate the energy of their soul even if many people will never understand the process, or will never have the possibility to recognize it. However, in order to renew our energy, we might need to *exfoliate* the dead cells, we must burn the negative remnants of our soul, such as deep hatred, destructive obsession, abuses, control over something we have no right to dominate. Obviously, this can be an internal struggle, between what we already have, we know, consider to be right, and the idea of eliminating, cleansing, cleaning the area and make place for something new.

The life on earth will exist with or without our personal problems or the ones of the country we live in. Unfortunately, so many of us, under desperate circumstances, might adopt a bad attitude, take unhealthy decisions, and consequently try to survive based on hidden actions that could damage the layers of the already wounded soul. Most of the time there might be a struggle, inflexibility, and objection. However, the internal conflict will only take place due to a lack of understanding at the moment. We all need this type of transformation to purify periodically our existence and nevertheless, to open the channels of the soul, in order to be able to nurture and heal it. Going forward, Pluto points the most important arc for a chart, both for individuals and countries. It is a crucial element for an individual's life. At social level the area where Pluto travels represents the hard work of that society, that country and it's important to move slowly and find a resolution for the issues in order to dissolve them. Hence, we might be true survivors only if we will follow the truth, otherwise, the entire process of living will be ruined, and we may have to repeat it somehow. Nevertheless, I would like to mention that Pluto through the houses could be split in two categories. The energy of these two categories is different because the intentions and the intensity might be different. So, for instance, when Pluto is in 1st to 6th houses, the intensity is more in terms of personal life, personal growth, money, communications, self-education, family, creation and everyday life routine. So, the individual passion could be emphasized in terms of private zone. People could bring things from the outside to improve and grow their private life.

On the other hand, when Pluto is transiting through the 7th to 12th houses then the intensity could have other connotations. The intense feelings could be in connection with the outside zone, outside that person's comfort zone. It may have to do with an exterior life area such as common investments, foreign countries, superior education, career, social projects in connection to others, hidden things, etc. This could also be the case for country charts. If Pluto will transit to the first six houses it might have to do with the internal zone, domestic issues. Then, if Pluto is transiting between 7th to 12th houses it might have to do with the outside zone, worldwide reputation, international law, connections and alliances, etc. Thus, throughout the course of my astrological journey, researching and analyzing directly charts, I have noticed how intense is Pluto when it transits a specific house. Moreover, Pluto will always opposite another house, so think about Pluto in transit as an axis. Pluto is doing investigations in one area of the chart, while automatically will be in opposition with another area of life. This opposite area will be out of control.

I have met many people that have Pluto in transit from 1st to 12th house, and I have a good idea what type of feelings Pluto transit could generate. Therefore, I will talk about Pluto significations through the houses, based on real stories.

Pluto Transiting the First House

With the support of computers, astrology could stimulate

and empower human civilization. In the same time, religions and psychology change tend to change our perception of the world around us. We are taught since we were little about so many things but how come we don't learn in school the most important thing, the *self*, and how to discover and how to get connected with the inner power?

The force of everything in the world could be the power of acknowledging and using the individual power. We all are like a small stone, small fractions from the Universe. We might have to learn our geological history, geological time scale, in order to understand the system of chronological measurement. What type of stone each one of us is? We have a fraction of energy, but how may we move that e-motion?

Thinking and asking such questions is symbolical, under Pluto influences. Pluto transiting through our 1st house could reset our inner power and hidden abilities to see the world from an intense point of view. Also, looking profoundly through the world, you may see it obscure. You may become interested in the hidden aspects of your character, identity. Symbolically, it might push you to learn about self-awareness, and perhaps it will open many unforgettable avenues. Pluto will analyze a hundred times each step you will put forward. Nevertheless, you might have that feeling of impossibility to move fast through the world. You could feel powerless. The low vibration, eventually, the discouragement, prepares you to embrace your spirit as first support. Hence, what you will discover during these years in your soul base could represent your most significant support for the future.

Pluto Transiting the Second House

Pluto will open many opportunities for you, to understand the meaning of life's values. As a first step you might look to increase your financial status on your own. You might attract money, wealthy people around. Many years you could open ways in terms of how to make money. You might have to choose the way you want to control your personal growth, your financial power.

Under each variation exhausting challenges may arise. Sometimes you could have an obsession to accumulate objects, to upgrade and change the condition of living. Pluto transiting your second house may put you in a place where the richest world that you have created is not helping you to move further. You could be still stuck in a point where life is challenging you, as if it would ask you to resist and play the game in a hidden manner.

Unfortunately, you might realize that your efforts mean nothing. It could come to a point where no matter how much money you have you realize you cannot buy things that cannot be bought like age, health, or life experiences that you have lost while you were focused on making money. If you realize this aspect in time, you might want to consider resetting your personal values, personal resource, and possessions.

Pluto Transiting the Third House

Despite all the 3rd house symbols, in my view, the 3rd house represents the inner voice; it's the language of our roots (very often we have IC in the 3rd house, too).Pluto through this zone could not be felt very well by the immediate environment. There could be a war zone in the early environment, and the person could secretly analyze and research short methods to communicate safety. Pluto offers us the richness that is embedded in what we think is most distasteful, such a hard effort, the pressure to control our thoughts. Pluto through the 3rd house might know better how to protect information, even how to deliver a secret message. Also, the person might be reserved in communications, and passionate obsessively with a particular topic. However, the person might have an inner force to re-examine many ideas, beliefs, plans, or everything in terms of knowledge, education, your childhood, early environment, siblings. The process could be slow, with rejections, but you could have your inside power that could transform the idea of communications, education, and learning language, even the early environment. Additionally, I have few cases of toddlers that have had Pluto in transit through the 3rd house/natal chart. They have had a delay in speech. I remember that the parents were afraid of autism. However, when I saw the Pluto transiting the 3rd house, I have recognized the slow movement of syllables.

Pluto Transiting the Fourth House

Each family may have their own theory on how to discover the mystery of living in power. Some families may transmit to their children the way of having dominant influences in their environment. So, you might have security, but you might not have freedom. The outside world is hard for so many people, but you did not catch the rhythm of the world, yet, because your parents suffocate you. They likely want to protect you but have obsessive control over you. They could give you a very good life platform, supporting you with the life directions, supplying you the resources you request, the connections you need, even your dream job. However, you might want desperately to "bite" that piece of world challenge.

It could be that you want to prove to yourself or your inner wishes to find your power in the world. The restriction to get out of your parental home is so intense, and nothing might compensate. You are unable to fully comprehend or to appreciate the effort of your parents because you never deal with pure reality. You were hidden, protected; all while your inner progress was likely blocked. During these years, you may want to escape from the tutelage of your parents. You are almost ready to give up and reboot your base. This is one possibility.

Another situation that I have found in several charts is adoption families. Kids that were adopted and protected by a new family that has somehow abused them, or they may feel deep pressure in that house. In another situation it could be that person who may divorce, and she/he have come back to live with her/his parents. They are living and develop their *power* under the power or "the family name",in the shadow of her/his parents.

Pluto Transiting the Fifth House

All of us have passions, inner creations, but most of the time, these inner qualities are not meant to be all ours. We have to recognize and develop them. Nevertheless, we may need to expose them to be useful for others. Unfortunately, we cannot fully control the inner quality that we grow. We, and our creations are part of the Universe, and our self-expression could reflect just a fraction of something. The most often examples that I have found of Pluto in the 5th house is the difficulty of conceiving a baby. No matter the effort, the treatment, or other facts, some things are not possible. In many cases, people may not accept this impossibility. The intensity could affect the soul harmonies and may disrupt its power. Very often this difficulty causes depression. Another example could be repetitively attracting inappropriate lovers. Consequently, the romance and the free time of the person in question was like a roller coaster, either passionate or even traumatized. Some elements of enjoying personal free time were eliminated, and the focus was towards the partner.

Other examples could be when you acknowledged the value of the activities you've been doing secretly over the years, such as writing poetry or painting. You have found a passion for the soul that reenergizes you each time the world's intensity puts you down. So, Pluto allows you to discover and secretly develop your inner treasures. Another case could be when a person is obsessed with a particular passion, self-expression, the way to create things in life, or even love affairs, games around joyful moments, perhaps wanting to demonstrate power.

Pluto Transiting the Sixth House

The world may move fast around you, and you could be lost in a particular passion, like when you want to discover something particular, profound, even if it is about tools, medicine or miraculous exercises that may transform yourself or others. On the other hand, you might voluntary investigate everything what seems wrong at your work place, in your job environment, like looking to separate the truth from the fake reality. You might have intense focus and passion for what you do in daily life.

The tension could be negative, too, and you may not like to be controlled or dominated by others, especially if they are not positive examples for you. So, you might develop negative obsessions with a particular colleague, boss, type of job, subalterns of you are in charge. You may understand the acting behind the human mask, and you may not have accepted it easily; an inner wish to change the job may develop. However, others might see you superficial or inefficient, but you might know exactly what are you looking for, and what you need for your life's redefinition, so you could not recognize your obsession and the motivation behind it. Nevertheless, watching the speed of others, you may understand generally the rhythm of life, and the meaning of transforming priorities during the everyday routine.

So, Pluto may investigate your daily routine, starting with your health, job, and diet program. Many things or people could be brushed out from your daily implications. On the other hand, during this time you could be more appreciated and supported by your boss, rather than your co-workers.

Pluto Transiting the Seventh House

A legal partner is someone that theoretically has to go in the same direction you go. It's like a shoe, it belongs to one pair, and both of them have to walk in the same direction. Pluto in the 7th house may create difficulty not only in finding the best partner but also in terms of commitment. The life may challenge your relationship, marriage until you redefine and transform the concept of the contractual partner, husband, and legal associate. In most of the cases that I have analyzed, one of the spouses struggle to understand the other one. The process of suffering alone seems to be the process of self-discovering through other people. Others, including your legal partner, husband, wife, could reject you and might push you in so many unfriendly ways. The meanings of these challenges seem to be predesignated, or you to find yourself in others; to understand your hidden potential; to have the capacity to control yourself and the actions of others towards you. You could put everyone in a big picture, and you may need to analyze what each person from your life wants from you, especially your spouse or life partner. You could follow the rules of your partner, or your inner strength could transform the dynamics of your relationship. As a result, you could generate and dictate a new set of life principles in terms of others and your deep relationship implication.

Pluto Transiting the Eighth House

During this transit, you may walk into a powerful corporation, institution, you could be around people that have some control, power, influent connections and you could even be around rich people. Maybe you may need to understand the power of money from others perspectives. At the same time, you may make money in connection with others, having a common investment. This is a simple example, but there are so many other possibilities under the 8th house. Under this section, I believe it's fair to share with you how I experienced it.

My Eighth House Transit Experience

Pluto transited the cusp of my 8th house, in June 2000, in Sagittarius, which is Jupiter's sign. My natal Jupiter is on the cusp of the 3rd, square Pluto. On July 1st, 2000, there was a Total Solar Eclipse (10° Cancer) that triggered my natal Jupiter, and the cusp of the 3rd house (short trip). On July 24th 2000, when Pluto transited the cusp of my 8th house, I was in a car accident. I had no major injuries, no broken bones, but I experienced a near-death experience that reconnected me to my purpose in life. So, the July eclipse activated Jupiter, the ruler of my 8th house. In addition, Jupiter was transiting my 1st house, which is also the house of the physical body. Somehow my body did not have major injuries, despite the impact. Symbolically, Jupiter protected my body and extended my life. At that time,

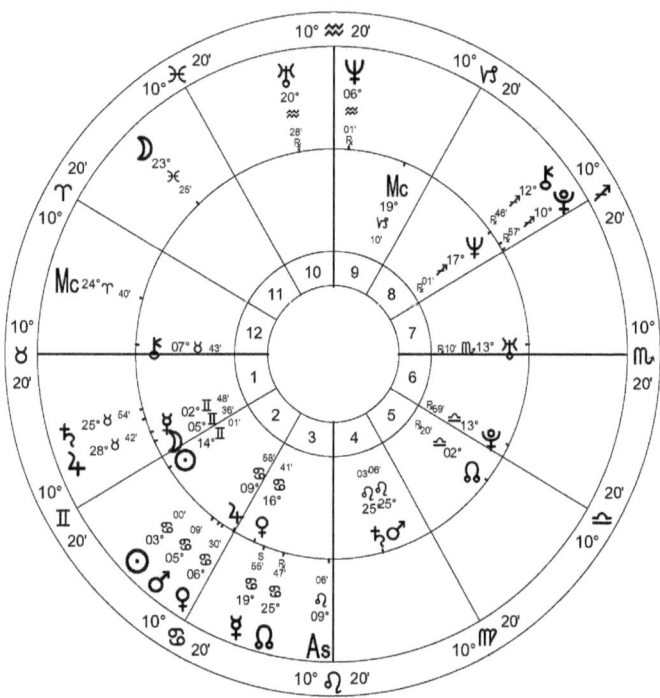

**Chart 39: Inner Wheel: Maria Stiopei natal: June 5, 1978, 2:55 AM; Sighetu Marmatiei, Romania; Equal House, Mean Node
Outer Wheel: Accident; July 24, 2000, 8:30 AM; Tandarei, Romania**

I briefly acknowledged that an impact was inevitable. In that second, I felt my soul left my body, I *melted* and slipped down to the floor (the driver's right seat). It was hard to understand how could I fit in there and in that way given my height (I'm 5' 7"). It was very hard for the paramedics to take me out from the wreckage. I had no pulse yet no broken bones and no major physical damages, just some scratches.

After that experience, I have redefined the life meanings, and secretly I have researched, investigating the concept of "after death" from philosophical perspectives. I felt as I had a choice to whether live or die. The meaning of my life at that time was for others, not for me. And I decided to live, to achieve my soul goal. At that time, Pluto in transit was in Sagittarius, activated the natal 8th house. After this near-death experience, I have continued my daily routines like before, but I always have had in my mind the reason why I have remained in this incarnation. Although I have understood my soul goal, I was unable to achieve it, because for me, at that time, the concept of helping human beings was to provide material support. I was a student, financially fully supported by my parents and working as a model. How can I help others?

Slowly, I have detached about that idea, and I continued to develop my life in the way I knew it at that time. However, my life directions were towards people. I have inner qualities to make easy connections and to stay connected to others. At that time I was the leader of all students, to the entire university. Notwithstanding, the open perspectives, the great support, during Pluto transiting over the natal 8th house, I have "died"; for the second time in the same life. Maybe because I have had the second chance to live, but I did nothing to achieve my soul wish, I chose to relocate. In a subtle way 'a love force' inspired me to withdraw from that reality. I have never dreamed of leaving far away from my country. None of my family members have lived at that time in another country, being very conservative and well-integrated into their environment.

Despite all the support I have received from wonderful parents, teachers, people who contributed positively to my growth, my soul needed something else, a real-world experience. Practically, I was "reborn" in the USA at a mature age. I had to start from a new beginning with everything again. My natal chart shows flexibility. Hence, it was easy to adapt to new circumstances, despite that I did not use my native language and I was not able to use my formal education. I had no support like I did back home. However, I have human values and an optimistic attitude. So, I was reborn (Pluto) like an orphaned person who has to reinvent and to survive at least the same quality of life that I had before. I have separated myself from others, by choice, and I was enthusiastic about understanding the philosophy of the world, from another angle. Moreover, I felt that my meaning was different than most of the immigrants.

Pluto Aftermath

I was *hard* on myself, and even with the people that had loved me the most. Also,my natal Neptune is in the 8th, which means sacrifices, losing others. I have assisted from a distance how, others died, grandparents, my dad, young cousin, teachers, and it was a painful feeling that made me understand that life is not what others want from us, instead is what we want from ourselves. Others nurture us, giving us the power to grow beautiful in the world, but not only around them. That might be a form of egoism. We might have to spread the sparkles of our root entities, to share with others our inner resources Also, I acknowledge that everything is part of our life cycle, and nobody dies at all; there is just regeneration. I also understand that nothing material can be valued, more than a feeling of soul fulfilment (Pluto transiting through the 8th house of values). Perhaps, the total abandon of my previous life and accepting my relocation, I have reconnected with the Universe power (Pluto transiting over my natal Neptune, 8th house). I have redefined my ideal, expanded it and I was able to access another alley of the mystical world (that I will prefer to talk about with another occasion).

Moreover, Pluto, in my case, eliminates everything that you can imagine associated with the 8th house, common material things, and heritage. Pluto during though a specific house, always prepares us for the next lesson. Symbolically, it has prepared me slowly, to detach entirely from the past, and to look further into the world. Pluto is transiting above the axis ASC-DES. So, in a very humble way, I let things go in the way the Universe took them from me. I comprehend both death and life transformation from a philosophical perspective. My life transformation was under Jupiter principles and I always feel protection from a divine force, no matter where I in the world I live. Pluto in the 8th house will teach us life's values. In fact, it's not about us, it's what can we bring from our inner treasure and add to the collective one.

Pluto Transiting the Ninth House

You may realize that you travel a lot, you have been connecting and learning elements from other cultures. Also, you might acknowledge that the philosophy of the world is different from your early environment. The concept you deliberately carry out based on a study, research, documentation might lift your beliefs. Pluto will peel off a layer of your world philosophy and will let you explore. When you are ready to proceed, you will have another opportunity to dig up another layer, and so on.

Slowly, you will go in a very distant direction, and automatically a possible conflict with the past may appear. You may become a master in your field during this time, if you studied intensely over the years. However, you could find yourself alone in the middle of the world, research program, for the sake of gaining wisdom. Your roots nurtured you to grow in such a way that you are worldly-wise. With or without intentions, maybe by your innocence or naivety, you have destroyed your early comfort to become a powerful stone in the world. The legends tell us that the most remarkable things that resist the test of time must be built on a strong stone, a sturdy foundation. However, at the other end of the road, your roots, siblings, your early environment, schools, relatives are still there. You might not be compatible anymore with the old life philosophy; also, the time has taken away the past generations like grandparents, uncles, and aunts. So, if you look back, there is not too much to find. Remember, several years ago, Pluto passed through your 8th house, perhaps has given you that passion to open "the world book".

This Pluto territory in transit could be the most difficult one, but maybe the most rewarded. Even if everything with *law* like the sister-in-law, mother-in-law, father-in-law, law in a country, the law as a dispute between brothers', all that which apparently obscures, can demoralize you. However, it's such a privilege to follow and learn based on self-experience, the road made by Pluto. Who follows its road, may serve his soul?

Pluto Transiting the Tenth House

You could be in a control position, such as a leader, but you could not have the popularity or the respect you crave at that time. In fact, you may have both of them, but the time moves so slow, that you don't see or notice there is any progress in your career. However, some of you might be tempted to leave that particular job, path or domain, believing that others may underestimate your methods of work. You may have a powerful ability to coordinate others, but unfortunately you could be limited by the CEO of the company you work for, or by peoples in a higher position than you. On the other hand, if the energy of inability to manage things in your own way is not well controlled there may be a temptation to over-control the subalterns. Despite the above, with patience, we can have the clarity to discover any hidden layer of no matter what career. What have you studied, researched several years ago? Where did you travel? That is the Pluto's natural path that you may want to follow. If you are in a different path symbolically Pluto may create difficulties and you could be determined to change the life direction. Also, we have to take in consideration that Pluto may transit the MC, too, and if the path was not in synchronicity with the inner wish, it a career or public life transformation may appear.

In my research, I have found several people that changed corporations, especially to stay and dominate the high position. Changing a corporation did not necessary eliminate future tensions and other types of control. Pluto may want us to dominate its energy and work through it.

Pluto Transiting the Eleventh House

You are outside of your private zone. You might realize that you have many wealthy, powerful friends in your social group that are like a part of your family. Some of them could open promising prospects to you. Together you could develop common ideals, have commune hopes, spend holidays together.

However, the platform of your social group will give you so many challenges that, at the end of all, you might realize that you have been manipulated. You could be used for various favours, such as a signature, loan, or corrupted matters, and as a consequence, years of recovery may follow. In other words, others could have specially created a favorable opportunity for you to help them later. Popularly, you were seduced to enter to the wealthy zone without any efforts.

This is just an example, but there are so many others. Think about the loyalty of many political figures. After releasing the new government positions, many "great and supporters" were excluded from the new political configuration, so they realized the betrayal of the group they thought they belonged to. Imagine you having a powerful social status. Because of that, you are invited to have a high government position that slowly attracts a lot of problems, just because you accepted to be associated with people with bad political reputation. However, after the culmination points of that crisis, you could find all the unseen connections that could put on hold unnaturally a commune ideal, collective interest, destroying commune hopes. At a positive level, this could upgrade the social international position.

Pluto Transiting the Twelfth House.

You may find yourself living in your own way, or you may reach a point in life were silence is very important. Maybe you are hiding a very intense secret, perhaps being ashamed of some inhuman action that others did to you. Your inner power could have been damaged, bothered unnaturally by external factors. You could hide some personal issues that somebody else has forced you into, even controlled you. This could be a young person who could have been raped and be ashamed to share their drama with others, keeping it hidden for years. Also, it could be about complicity, or other things that somebody saw, hear or did; and the things that are hidden carefully today, might disturb intensely the inner power of that person.

Another example could be even in terms of death. Let's say three best friends travel in a car, one of them died in the car crash, but the people who survive will never tell the truth, like to cover the other friend who was the driver. Pluto in the 12th house may be the perfect place to hide, and the may be an option where to retreat or escape: institutions, hospitals, monasteries or meditation, or other ways of personal controlled way of cleaning away what poisoned your subconscious. Pluto is researching a way of transformation through the house where it is transiting, meaning that it is directly looking for those hiding layers that were remained unseen by even us, or our society. We are all the times invisible under a period of redefinition, regeneration, but we may have not the clarity to comprehend the meaning of that life moment and what that life moment wants to teach us. Only after Pluto leaves a particular section of life, we might look back, and we could understand the meaning of everything we have experienced in that specific time.

Of course, we may be able to find meaning in that life lesson if we are open to understand those circumstances. Additionally, Pluto in transit shows us how slow the dying process is developing, what zone of our life could be burned in a such a way that nothing can be safe, perhaps just the land, the soul, de spirit, that could be reinvented again.

CHAPTER FOUR
Pluto Transiting the Charts of Countries

"The political horoscope may be perceived as the window through which the astrologer may see the condition of the society at any one time. It is also, of course, a map of the political life of the society. It is also clear that the national chart may represent the culmination of a series of processes in the life of the state as much as it represents the beginning of a new order."

Nicholas Campion -
The Book of World Horoscopes

Pluto influences are associated with the most important changes in the World. Pluto marks human history. We, as a society, can recognize generally the particular tension that our country is struggling with. However, only when Pluto activates a natal Planet (1°orb), or a significant point such as an angle, house or cusp, does the society feel the intensity of their nation's problems. This is especially felt when Pluto is in aspect with Saturn, because Saturn represents the structures of the countries, government and organizations, and Pluto might disturb the traditional form of holding things under control. So, for instance: the beginning of World War I (28 July 1914) has degenerated from a military conflict with a worldwide dimension. At that time Pluto had just entered Cancer, which is a sign of social security, human protection, and global population. However, on June 23, 1914, just one month before the first war started, there was a New Moon (1°18" Cancer), falling over Pluto (0°39" Cancer), within a 1-degree orb. The decision to start a war could have been triggered around this time. The war had been developing while Pluto was in conjunction with Saturn, in the same degree (2° Cancer), a cardinal, water sign. Then, Pluto - Saturn travelled together, in a very close orb and they both were retrograde in October 1914.Consequently, the statistics show that during 1914-1918 the most soldiers' fatalities took place.

Another example would be at the end of July 1947 when Saturn came very close to Pluto, and starting with August 1947, Saturn was in the same degree as Pluto (12° Leo). It was the culmination point of this conjunction. Leo is the second fire sign, having fixed modality. The history tells us that around this time the following evens took place:

- On August 15, 1947, India became an independent country.
- On August 4, 1947, Argentina and Ireland established full diplomatic relations.
- On August 5, 1947, 35 Zionist leaders in Palestine were detained for terrorist activities; Pluto is very often associated with terrorism, secret methods to control a type of power and organized hidden crimes. Also, it may be associated with threats and ruthlessness.
- On August 10, 1947, General Lucius D. Clay reported the release of the last 8 million German prisoners of war and the complete destruction or conversion of all armament plants in the US-occupied zone. The United States became the first of the four occupying powers to release all of its German POWs.
- On August 15, 1947, Britain's first atomic reactor started up at Harwell.
- On August 30, 1947, about 90 people were killed and 60 injured in a movie theatre fire in the Ruel district of Paris, France. There are so many important events around this time that may symbolically correlate with Pluto's influences.

Another period was the beginning of November 1982. At that time Pluto was conjunct Saturn at 27° Libra. During July 1981– November 1982 there was an economic downturn triggered by tight monetary policy in an effort to fight mounting inflation. Although goods producers accounted for only 30 percent of total employment at the time, they suffered 90 percent of job losses in 1982. In terms of the future, even if Pluto might mark significant events of a particular country, things cannot be manifested without the human input. However, there seems to be a correlation between the needs of a society and the leaders who could represent the society's needs. So, in this sense, it will be important to analyze the leader of the world and the time in question.

How are the leaders of the world nowadays, as human beings? Their charts could define and delimitate their social ideals and their personal vocations. Also, the countries charts show details about domestic interest as well as international influences. Below, I will enumerate a few examples of Pluto transiting over the natal chart of countries. Note where the arc of Pluto starts and where is going. Each generation seems to have a new opportunity to slightly progress their organization in their country.

Despite the enthusiasm of new generations of politicians, a country redefinition means a full understanding of the past; in the sense of taking over and rectifying. Pluto eliminates and rebirths the social passion of a society, powerful organizations, etc. Therefore, a healthy transformation might never come fast, but in a very slow motion. A fast transformation may come only under a death process, like social movements, revolutions and war. In other words: a forced way of cancelling and destroying the past.

From the following examples, you can see the activated zone of regeneration, the main area of the intense struggle of a nation and how the process of redefinition might manifest from an astrological point of view.

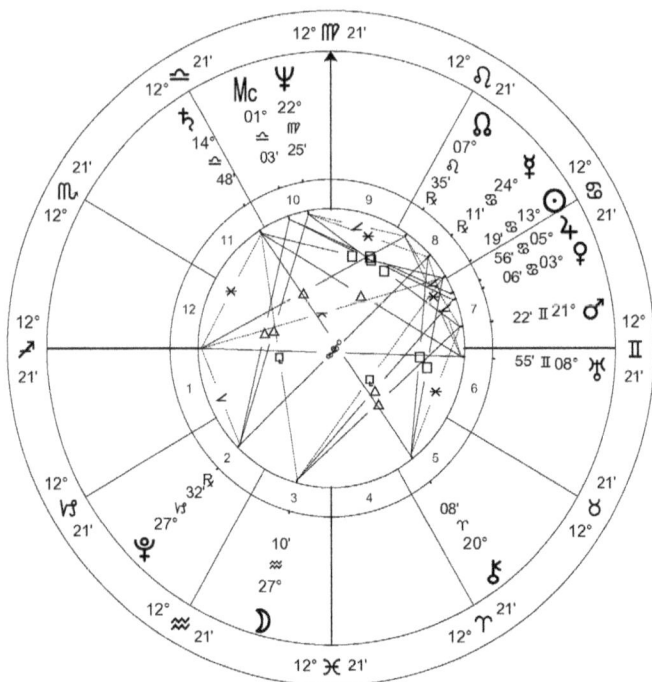

Chart 40: Natal Chart of the USA
July 4, 1776, 5:10 PM; Philadelphia, Pennsylvania

The United States

Briefly, the USA natal chart shows a stellium in Cancer, involving Sun–Jupiter- Venus. So the Sun and Venus accompany the ruler of the chart, Jupiter. Cancer is the sign of security, nurturing, population, and Jupiter conjunct Venus emphasizes generosity, supporting feminism, highlighting human values, etc. On the other hand, there are no traditional planets in earth elements, just Pluto and Neptune, so they could represent important keys to align with the real things in the world. Nevertheless, Pluto is where we have the potential to feel and be powerful, so the 2nd house could suggest an invisible power of position,

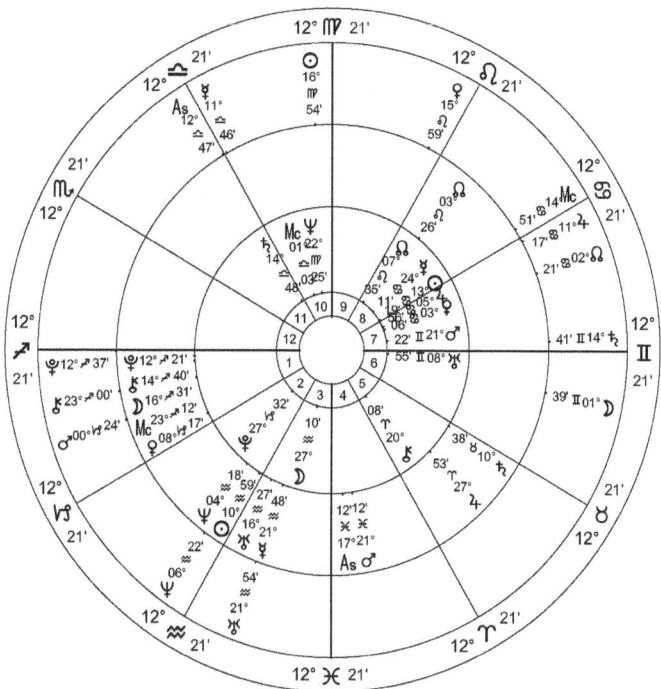

Chart 41: Pluto transits 2000/01 over USA
Inner Wheel: Natal Chart of the USA
Middle Wheel: January 31, 2000, 8:46 AM; New York, New York
Outer Wheel: September 9, 2001, 8:46 AM; New York, New York

money, tools that may dominate and support the dynamic of the country. Natal Pluto is in Capricorn (2nd) trine Neptune in Virgo (10th), and the MC in Libra (10th). In contrast, Pluto opposes Mercury in Cancer (8th), suggesting a significant conflict between individual growth, the domestic abundance of the country and discussions on matters of sharing information and knowledge with others.

If we look back in time over the chart of the USA, we will see that at the end of January 2000, Pluto was exactly over the Ascendant (Sagittarius 12° 21"), suggesting a rebirth of the nation, profound changes in the sense of national identity. The redefinition could have started with a cold view towards the natural path of the country; a process of crisis that could have expanded the wisdom of the nation especially in terms of common growth and accumulation. We might feel the intensity; the pressure and we can struggle at the moment pointed out by a culmination aspect, but the result could be seen after the volcano has erupted. During the year 2000 Pluto moves back and forth over the ASC. At last, on August 23rd, 2001, Pluto moved direct and slowly prepared to separate from the Ascendant. However, on September 9th, 2001, Pluto in transit was still conjunct Ascendant (12°37" Sagittarius). The first house can represent national identification, new beginnings, and outer appearances-approach.

Additionally, on September 9, 2001, Pluto had transited over the Ascendant, Sagittarius, which is Jupiter's sign. At that moment, Jupiter in transit activated the cusp of the 8th house, which is the natural house of Pluto. Then, if we follow the slow movement of Pluto, we will see that on February 2014, it has transited over the cusp of the 2nd house (domestic financial matters, money). The statistics shows that in early 2014 there was a significant drag on the economy, disrupting production, construction, and shipments, and deterring home and auto sales. U.S. GDP Dropped 2.9% In the First Quarter 2014, Down Sharply from Second Estimate.

The Bureau of Economic Analysis released its third and final estimate of real gross domestic product for the first three months of 2014. The release showed output in the U.S. declining at an annual rate of 2.9 per cent" (see Chart 41). It's fascinating how well the chart's aspects are synchronized and coincide with what happened in the USA in the last approximately 20 years. When we comprehend the astrological aspects in correlation with social manifestations, then we might have an idea about the future.

Going forward, Pluto in transit will come very close to Pluto's natal position (27° Capricorn) at the end of April 2021. Pluto in transit will reach 26°48" Capricorn, and then it will turn ret-

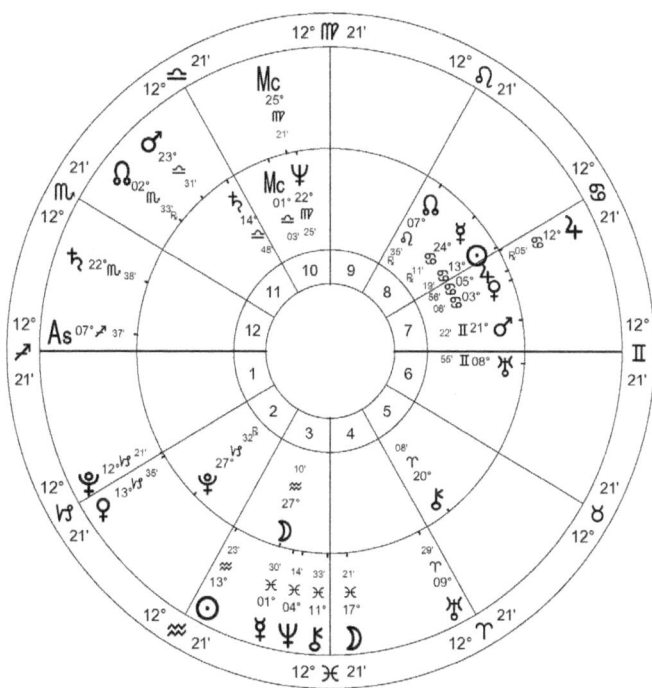

Chart 42: Pluto transits over USA Fenruary, 2014
Inner Wheel: Natal Chart of USA
Outer Wheel: February 2, 2014, 2:49 AM, New York, New York

rograde. However, at the beginning of February through middle of March 2022, Pluto in transit will be in a perfect conjunction with natal Pluto (27° Capricorn). This culmination point might have an impact on USA, pinpointing a zone that is already in a slow process of suffering. This area of the nation could require redefinition, transformation in some way. If we will take into consideration the USA chart with a Sagittarius Ascendant (12°21") than the impact may be in terms of the 2nd house, meaning monetary system, values and resources of the nation, security, everything in terms of material stability, the concept of traditional form of property and possessions in general. If for the past generations,

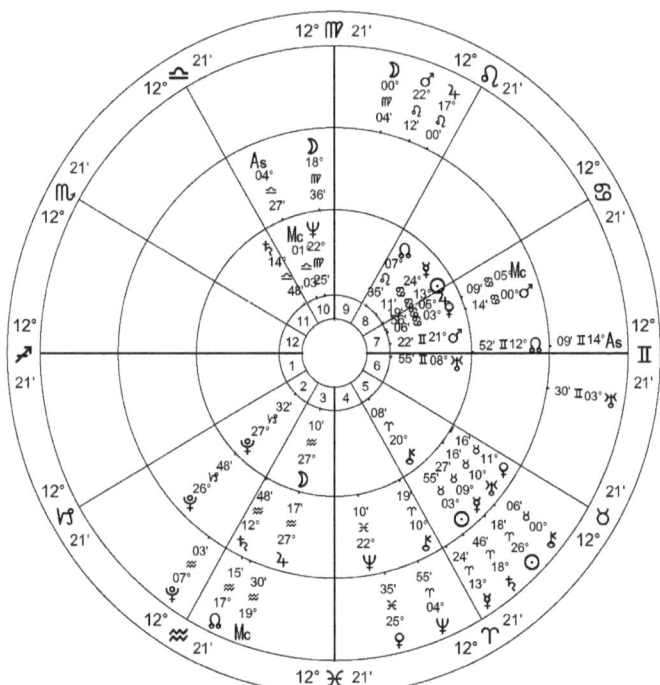

Chart 43: Pluto transits over USA Chart 2021/2027
Inner Wheel: Natal Chart of the USA
Middle Wheel: April 23, 2021, 5:10 PM; New York, New York
Outer Wheel: April 16, 2027, 8:46 AM, New York, New York

the USA has focused in terms of building powerful international connections, now, as you can see, Pluto transiting below the ASC-DSC axis requires focus on the domestic area, internal development, improvement, increasing the security of the country and desire to increase the material possibilities of the nation.

On the other hand, if the national chart shows transformation relating to the 2nd house, then who is the party or the presidential candidate that offers things that are in synchronicity to the concerns mentioned above? Could he or she be the magnet, the force that attracts the society? No matter how powerful a nation's chart can be, nothing will move without human decisions and power. The collective consciousness seems to push to the surface the person who represents them the most. Then, what if we will go further following Pluto transits? The next national challenges might be when Pluto in transit activates the nodal axis, respectively when Pluto conjuncts the S Node in Aquarius (7°35"/ 2nd house) and is opposite N Node in Leo (7°35" / 8th house). The culmination point will be at the beginning of April 2027, and it might be felt strongly during May 2027, too. Moreover, another impact of domestic issues could start in May 2030, when Pluto will transit over the cusp of the 3rd house (12°21 Aquarius). Of course, Pluto never works alone, so it will depend on the rest of the aspects to understand the predispositions and the complex picture of a future time.

The United Kingdom

Briefly, the United Kingdom natal chart shows structures, conservationism and practical energy with the initiative to lead and take actions. Also, the chart suggests the vocation of the country as being reputable, respected among other countries. The information and international connections seem to be naturally very well analyzed, controlled, limited, perhaps using superior, old methods to comprehend how the rest of the world is organized and how other countries function practically. (Mercury/ Saturn is in a mutual reception. Mercury is conjunct the Sun and also the MC in Capricorn (9th). Moreover, Mercury is part of Earth Grand Trine involving Saturn (5th) and Neptune (1st) suggesting a high degree of harmony in terms of those three houses, respectively: the importance of focusing on independent growth, creating their own structures as methods to follow in order to be noticed in the world's eyes, and to have international authority and distinctions. Previously, I mentioned about Mercury, because it seems to have a very important role in the Brexit referendum that took place on the June 23, 2016 in the United Kingdom and Gibraltar. The succeeding government initiated

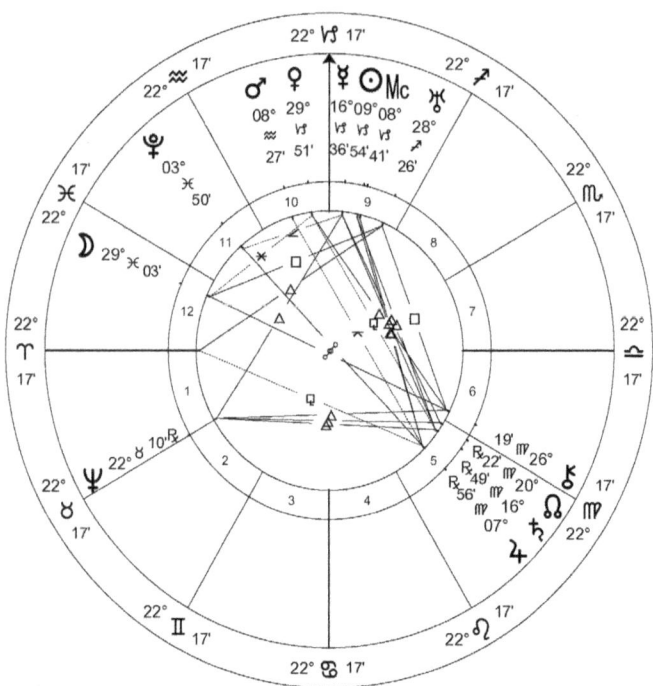

Chart 44: Natal Chart of the United Kingdom
December 25, 1066, 12:00 PM; Westminster, England

the official EU withdrawal process on March 29, 2017, and the negotiation period was later extended until January 31, 2020. Additionally, Mercury symbolically may represent siblings, connections and bringing people or ideas together. In a nation's chart Mercury could represent a sibling's country that are part of a big family, such as the EU.

If you follow Pluto's transits you will see that on June 23, 2016, Pluto was in a perfect conjunction with natal Mercury (16°36') in the 9th house, actually activating the natal Earth Grand Trine (Please see the Chart 45, Middle Wheel and Inner Wheel). The voice, the majority message of the country could have requested

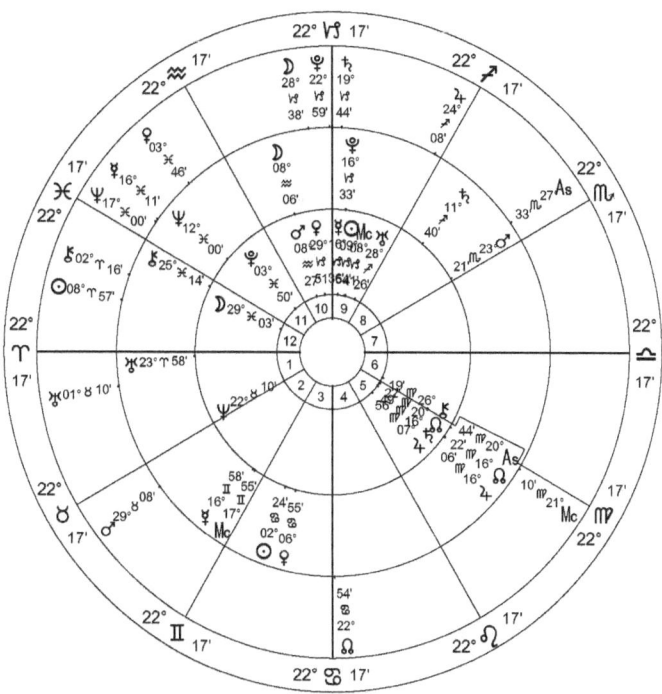

Chart 45: Pluto Transits over the United Kingdom
Inner Wheel: Natal Chart of the United Kingdom
Middle Wheel: June 23, 2016, 12:00 PM; London, U.K.
Outer Wheel: March 29, 2019, 11:00 PM; London, U.K

redefinition after a long process of the international dissatisfaction, limited or legal slow development. Consequently, the social movement could slowly terminate people in political power to destroy some important diplomatic relationships, disputing their rights with the parents of this formal organization (EU) separating the country from other nations, and demanding new, superior perspectives.

So, the old form of dealing with other countries such as foreign trade, practical methods of negotiation, commerce, and transporta-

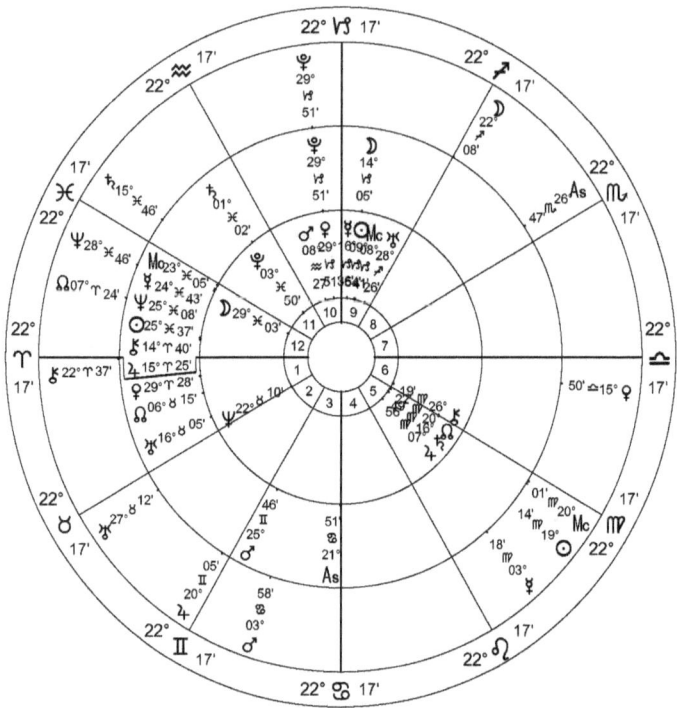

Chart 46: Pluto Transits over the United Kingdom
Iner Wheel: Natal Chart of the United Kingdom
Middle Wheel: March 16, 2023, 12:00 PM, London, U.K.
Outer Wheel: September 11, 2024, 12:00 PM, London, U.K

tion/ shipping might have to strategically end, or drastically transform in order to redefine the authority, rules and law of the country; refreshing its principles and philosophy. Nevertheless, the ending of the old international trade might bring not just separation from the EU, but it might have noticeable consequences, as well.

Going forward, in March 2023 Pluto in transit will be in a perfect conjunction with natal Venus (29° 51" Capricorn), in the 10th house. Pluto will go back and forth because of ret-

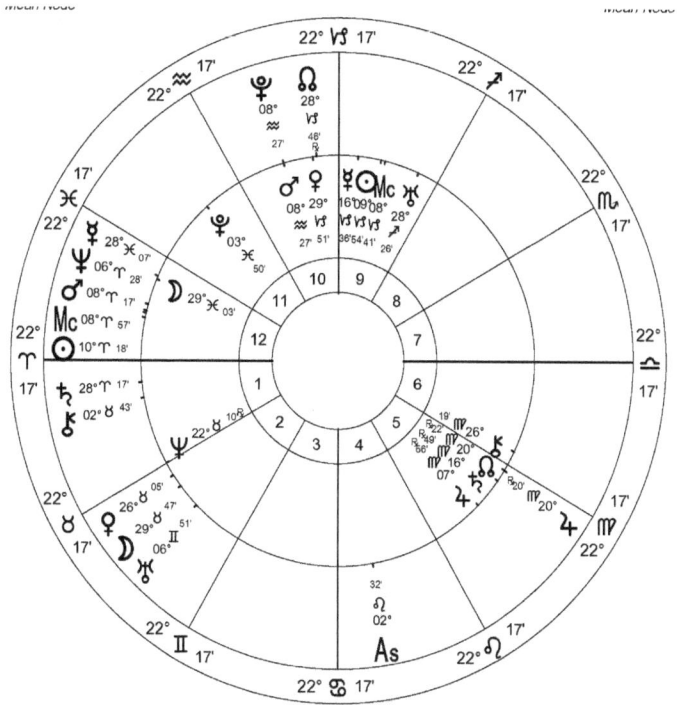

Chart 47: Pluto Trnsits over the United Kingdom
Inner Wheel: Natal Chart of the United Kingdom
Outer Wheel: March 30, 2028, 12:00 PM, London, U.K

rograde motion, while in September 2024, Pluto will again be in a perfect conjunction with natal Venus. Pluto represents the slow process of death, redefinition of power, total transformation, while Venus represents a female figure, diplomacy, peace, harmony and love, arts and culture, the entertainment industry.

So, during the above period, UK may reach a culmination point, an important event that might be written in the UK history. It could become a popular subject for the nation and be noticed all across the world.

On March 2028 Pluto in transit will come to a perfect conjunction with natal Mars (8°27" Aquarius, in the 10th house). Mars is the ruler of the UK chart. Pluto in transit will go backward and forward because of retrograde motion. Hence this aspect will last and continue during 2029, too. However, on May 9th, 2028, Pluto will turn direct over the same degree of natal Mars (8°49 Aquarius). So, this planetary intersection might highlight a young male that will be recognized as someone with courage and a brave spirit – a young leader, a popular and public figure of the country (Royal circle) that shows influence over the country.

In addition, Mars is associated with accidents, danger, heat, aggression, murderers, dangerous tools such as knives, guns, weapons of all kinds, soldiers, and points to war, explosions, the armed forces, military bases and military governments. On the other hand, Pluto shows death, regeneration. Moreover, Pluto transits will pass over natal Mars multiple times. In astrology, we call them "hits." Therefore Pluto will have multiple hits over natal Mars. The last time when transiting Pluto will pass over natal Mars (the last hit) will be on December 2029. (For more clarity you can go back and see Chapter Two / Pluto in Collaboration with Mars.) Additionally, the Pluto–Mars connection in air, in the fixed sign Aquarius might suggest sudden and unexpected trouble, death and pressure on the Monarch; suggesting an energy that emphasizes a challenging circumstance for the country; it could show brutality, rebels, turbulence in the country/Monarchy, Government. This period could be the beginning of a new session. Is possible for UK to redefine their army; to rebirth a new innovator and high, intelligent forms of defence.

Countries are like people. Are all countries going in the same direction that the world requires? If not, in what way and why is a nation "different", and what is that country's view? We have so many examples of how Pluto collaborates, and the way Pluto acts. It's that power, that if you don't it use for the purpose it has been created, could degenerate in a very destructive way. When we talk about Pluto, we have to take in consideration Pluto as power of the world. The leaders of the world nowadays have Pluto supported by different platforms that may confirm for us that they control different principles as well as they rule over different generations, with different principles of power. Despite this, each of them has Pluto somehow emphasized in their natal chart. This highlights how they build their power, which is supporting it and most importantly how they will use it.

Pluto could reveal the secrets of any country of interest or any powerful organization. For more details that could lead to complex results, we will need to analyze the eclipses (countries of interest and their leaders), the ordinary lunations, great conjunctions, and the political events to understand the social trend.

"Mundane Astrology is a most intricate and difficult branch of science, but it has its compensations". I believe my Pluto method can bring a new understanding of the world's manifestation and better clarity for the future of any country or powerful organization, etc. For those who don't know, The Ancients divided Astrology into "Doctrine of the Nativity" (also called Genethlialogy), Judicial Astrology (Horary), and Mundane Astrology.

Charles E. O. Carter.
An Introduction to Political Astrology

CHAPTER FIVE

Pluto in a Powerful Organization's Chart

"Pluto forces us to find our own inner values and resources, and radically transform the way we relate."

The Astrology Place

Pluto may have a crucial role in each powerful organization's chart, as well as in the leaders of those organizations. Pluto symbolizes power and each organization's objective is in one way or another to dominate, to control some attributes. I may not have the correct birth information for NATO's chart, an example that I used below. However, I leave the subject open for you to think about the possibilities of Pluto in transits over such a powerful worldwide alliance. It could show the deeper purpose (even secret purpose) of the organizations and nevertheless the tendencies or what challenges may come along on the way.

NATO, which was formed in 1949, is the most powerful military alliance in the world. Currently twenty nine countries are members of NATO.

Briefly, in NATO's chart, Pluto is part of Fire Grand Trine that emphasizes the 11th, 7th and 3rd houses. Pluto is in Leo, 11th, trine Mercury, Mars, Venus, and Sun in Aries, 7th. Pluto activates the stellium, controlling positively the power of everything that is associated with a war platform, respectively: actions, partnerships, ideas of leading others, and intelligence.

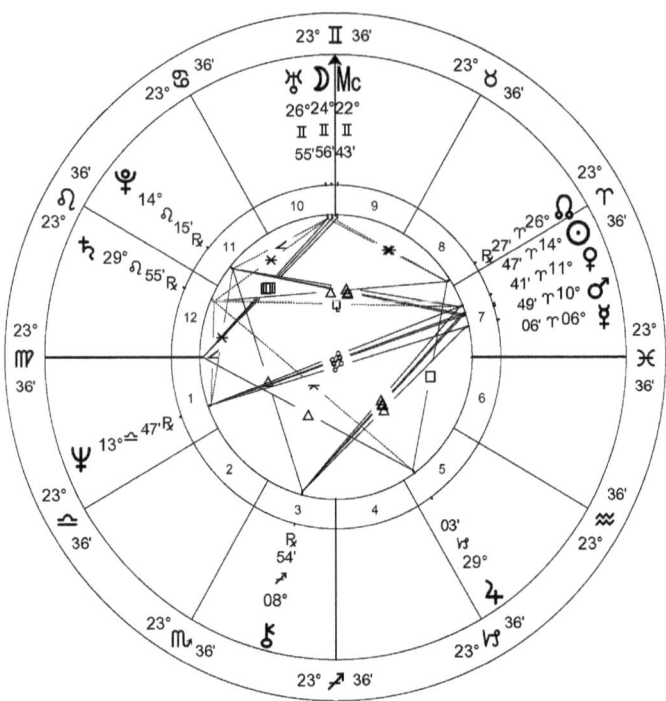

Chart 48: Formation of NATO: April 4, 1949, 4:45 pm; Washington, DC

From an astrological perspective, communications and relationships are vital for NATO. Mercury is the ruler of the chart and part of the stellium in 7th, also trine both Chiron in the 3rd house of communications and Pluto in the 11th house of international partnership, commune ideals. Hence, there seems to be a natural positive way to control and accompany the dynamic in the inner cycles. Despite this, there may be a challenge in the NATO zone that emphasizes the not easily reconciled communication, information, and knowledge zone. It's like "the siblings" nations that are in NATO members are not entirely healed from the past historical conflicts.

So, this may affect the movement to expand worldwide, powerfully. If we go back in time, we will see that Pluto in transit passed over the Ascendant (23°36" Virgo) multiple times, on October 11, 1968, March 21, 1969, the last time on August 11, 1969. So, around this period there may have been some historical events that could've slowly transformed the energy (meaning) of this powerful military alliance. Also, in August 1969, transit Chiron conjunct natal Mars (6°Aries, 7th). Moreover, transit Mars conjunct natal Chiron (8°54" Sagittarius).

The history of NATO between 1968-1969 shows that, October 17, 1968 – Signature in Prague of legal agreement authorizing temporary stationing of Soviet troops in Czechoslovakia. November 14-16 1968 – Ministerial Meeting of the Council in Brussels. The Ministers denounce Soviet actions in Czechoslovakia as contrary to the basic principles of the United Nations Charter and give a warning to the USSR. They decided to improve the state of NATO defense forces, confirm they will continue to study possibilities of détente, and the indispensable necessity of the Atlantic Alliance.

Pluto transiting over the ASC may be associated by a reborn new idea in terms of controlling the power. At that time, it has expanded into an alliance of fifteen countries. Consequently, during that time, NATO could have shown restructuring the principles that the alliance has had to follow. Also, if we will look further to Pluto transits over the NATO chart we will see that in December 1976 Pluto passed for the first time over natal Neptune (13° Libra, 1st), revaluating the ideal of the alliance, eventually making some progress and contribution to the general prosperity of the alliance, especially in matters of diplomacy, the art promoting co-operation.

Then, in December 1981, transit Pluto has activated the nodal axis, by conjunct South Node (26°27" Libra), respectively opposite North Node (26°27" Aries). The NATO historical events show: The North Atlantic Council met in Ministerial Session in

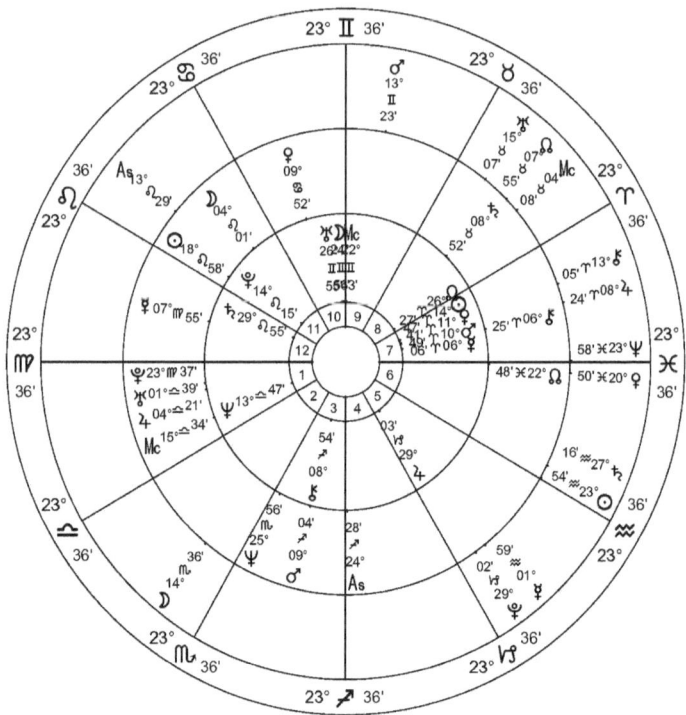

Chart 49: Pluto transits 1969/2023 over NATO chart
Inner wheel: NATO: April 4, 1949, 4:45 PM, Washington D.C.
Middle Wheel: August 11, 1969, 4:45 PM
Outer Wheel: February 12, 2023, 4:45 PM

Brussels on December 10 and 11 1981. On this occasion Ministers signed the Protocol of Accession of Spain to the North Atlantic Treaty.

Additionally, in February 2023, Pluto in transit will conjunct natal Jupiter (29°03,"5th) for the first time (see Chart 48). This may show expanding power after a long term of hard work involved. Nevertheless, other important aspects support these aspects that I have mentioned above. This example is just the idea of how Pluto could show the progress of alliance with everything involving it: challenge, transformations, ideal regenerations and long-time purpose.

There are so many powerful organizations like The United Nations (ONU), The European Union (EU), The Organization of Islamic Cooperation (OIC), and many more. It will be interesting to analyze each of them separately and then connect them to see their dynamic. Pluto is like a station that will evaluate our soul periodically, or the power of the country, alliance, organizations base of actions.

There is a small radius from 360 degrees of our life zone manifestation, where we might be screened in the way our generation wants to, or the next generation will learn about our age. In my view, Pluto is like a mine. We must go down each time we want to understand the roots of the precious stones. There may be no light to point out the route we have to take. We might have to discover our way to see things, and also, we might want to decide what we want to see and feel, the coldness, the heavy air?

Once we go in the dark, the mystery offers us so many reach points. Perhaps at that point, it is just the precious stones that shine to be noticed. Also, it could be collected and might be placed on a wire as a chain symbol of "the human soul." Moreover, each of the stones is unique same as each existence on the Earth is unique, too. Consequently, we, as human beings, are all connected on the same wires name it by Me 'the human evolution'. All the stones that are shine in the dark could be noticed for sure. We, as humans, are too greedy not to notice what is valuable.

I think humanity always needs something distinctive in the world environment, in order to develop new things as generations and progress on the evolutionary scale. We might be responsible as individuals for our own evolution, but we as humans are responsible for the evolution of our generations, too. If we will not be well prepared to detect what is unique in the world, then it's possible to not be able to recognize the originality of something valuable for our generation. Without progress, our generation could pause or could delay the steps of evolution. This is why I called group karma and it could be under Pluto's influences. Symbolically, the outer planets, including Pluto might show this type of 'group Difficulty'.

Perhaps each big organization, country might have "group karma". In fact, we are all under some social rules and principles. Some of the actions, the principles of a country at one point in time could be grateful for its generation, but it maybe not be good, or even harmful for the world's interest, for human beings in general. We have separated ourselves as humans in groups, societies countries, even if we all are the same.

In essence, we have been divided into groups, society, countries for better administration; the better of us to lead and handle the people in the way of helping them to progress on their evolutionary progress. Hence, even if the root of this idea seems to be good, in practice it seems to be split, and nowadays could not correlate with the world morality.

All in all, natal Pluto invites us to unfold gradually layers by layers of our inner soul, while in transit, pushing us hardly towards progress. In other words, future progress and our human evolution always depend on our depth. Hence, the connections that Pluto makes in the natal chart show the base, while what is in the transit's chart is the map (directions). As mentioned previously, this is valid for countries and leaders of the world charts. How deep we go may show how much further we might see. The present is the balance of past and future. We all live in our own private and social circles.

A Final Note to My Readers

I wish you all a meaningful life, full of mature love, kindness, generosity, and compassion. We all are connected, and each of us has a unique role in this life, in this universe. Grow your spirit in the way of blessing peace. The world is superficial. Not many people live the existence deeply. No matter how our life is, in the end, all of us will die. We will have multiple times a possibility to change our identity in the world, our values. We might need to be open to redefine our priorities to have a more fruitful existence.

In the end, the soul is the center of who we are; it is essential. Our souls exist before we were born and will exist after we die. The character reflects our soul, while the personality is just the trend of our temporal existence on the earth. As you can see, the skeleton of the future is not a secret at all. It's hidden in the Universe configurations. It requires self-scarification, and a total detachment from the material world to unfold a path that conducts the spirit from where it came; to translate the Universe's dynamic for the rest of people. The Universe is reflected in us.

References

The source of the examples that I have used is astro.com and Wikipedia.

CHAPTER SIX

Saturn-Pluto Conjunction with Jupiter Transiting

A similar article to this was published in 2019, by the AFA (American Federation of Astrologers), in their magazine, Today's Astrologer,volume 81,issue 5.

Each of us, with no exception, symbolically have Pluto somewhere influencing our life cycle. Thus, every day, Pluto transits a specific section of the natal chart. Pluto is, in effect, the 'second,' that passes in a year, while making us feel deeply the source of every moment in our lives. Thus, the mysteries of the soul begin to 'break out' slowly while we become strongly connected with intense feelings. For various reasons however, we could keep these feelings secret, hence in the shadows.

Consequently, and without intent, we may all have assembled a minefield inside us. Thus, our soul seems to be incapable of doing something, because what we *desperately* wish for depends, in some way, on external factors. We, as souls, are locked in this human existence. Even if we possessed the power, and the control over it, we cannot simply escape; thus, we have to experience particular circumstances. Perhaps, we may want to 'dig deep' into our past in order to comprehend the meaning and purpose of our soul in our current incarnation Some of us may have to bury our anger, our emotions, and even our passions —

those things may remain until the time is right for them to be brought into the light. Eventually, we may have to *recharge* our energy cells in order to survive.

Pluto's Evolutionary Preferences

Symbolically, Pluto *clings* to our soul through a specific life cycle. Pluto forces us to accept life as it is; it forces us to move forward with our lives — even if the moment has become lethargic. Moreover, Pluto may push us into transforming that part of our existence which we consider to be *dead*. Despite everything we do, the outside world may not favour our actions. Actually, Pluto will let us burn very slowly until we feel how *insignificant* we are in this world. It's not about humiliation; its merely a thoughtful lesson to see the vibration from the underworld. Each of us, with no exception, may have to deal with something profound in our lives, and no one else can go through these particular experiences that are unique to us — no matter their social status.

In some cases, we might be forced to go nowhere, but to meet our physical death. Furthermore, here regeneration is producing a new force of energy, which can transform the entire concept of that *something* that has slowly *burned* us for years. We will understand that nothing is without reason, and the slow movement we have to endure in a specific life cycle makes us learn that underworld lesson. It is similar to the wisdom which has been born from struggle. In time, we will understand the silence, the darkness, the coldness, and the mystery of the underworld. Similarly, it's like touching the ground with your ear in order to hear the language of the underground — an *echo* of another time. Thus, you comprehend everything, because in Pluto's domain, you learn everything on your own. Perhaps the light of your soul will penetrate deep into the ground — allowing your mind to perceive and investigate every layer of the dark world. However, at this stage of exhaustion, imagine a superior teacher; perhaps a school inspector who walks into your school.

Thus, he may have to evaluate the individual level of learning, or maybe the entire school.

We ask ourselves, what is the inspector looking for? What is the meaning of the evaluation? Those who studied the hardest will understand everything, the purpose of the examination, and what the answers should be. Everyone, without exception, might face some sort of evaluation around January 2020. Of course, with a different subject — intensely from person to person. However, what if this is not about school evaluations, what if this is about world evaluations? What if the internal pressure of those in need created an invisible force? What if this force explodes at any moment? What if no one listened to helpless people around the world? Moreover, what if the *inspector* of our existence wants to evaluate our resisting force, our patience and discipline in regard to time, soul passion, life structure, and morality?

In simple terms, I see the Saturn-Pluto conjunction as a long-term lesson — complete with hidden pressures — as to the limits of intensity of holding — the discipline and underappreciation — the real world and the mysterious world — the fears and the intimidation — as they collide with the masters who control the real power. In addition, many of us could give up easily, because we as humans, have the temptation to give up before we should, to separate from rigidity, inconvenience, and simple hard work. Many of us have already left that 'slow down life process,' hence the journey of transformation, without thinking about the benefits of our hard labor. So, maybe some of us prematurely give up the chance of soul purification, and the freedom concerned with human existence. In other words, we *poison* our fundamental hopes and passions. Hence, the intensity we cannot resist holds for us a very profound feeling of frustration, and a fear for the future. We can, however, bury it in a layer of mysticism, and then attach it as a deep secret in our soul. However, carrying secrets makes it difficult to exist, and hard to live.

However, what if you refuse to give up, and you continue to reinvent yourself as a result — providing continuity to your life? There is an old saying, "what can't kill you will make you stronger." So, in this case, your life force can grow stronger, and you may also become more resistant. As a result, you could see everything through a different perspective. Perhaps, your entire life principles will begin to change. Your life structure could be rebuilt. Your priorities may also change. Consequently, others may control your physical interactions, but nobody can control the power within your soul. So, you could die a hundred, or even a thousand times; but you can be *reborn*; and a million times more powerful.

Pluto's Evolutionary Power

More than that, at this particular juncture in your life, you can demonstrate that you are capable of holding the life forces in the same way, as you press the button of death, and the power of staying alive — without joy or light in your life. It's almost as if you are a valuable friend to everyone — even the Lord of Darkness. Your soul will have been gradually transformed — with your power of vision. You are the lucky one! From now on, you are optimistic, or at least your knowledge of life has transformed. The universe may want you to expand upon your life, and your happiness. Thus, you are rewarded, and you deserve it. (You may recognize the symbols of Jupiter here, because Jupiter configures on this Saturn-Pluto conjunction). Jupiter will be the best judge ever.

The power of the universe may bring you an additional benefit. Perhaps, you will have a new teacher in your life? Or maybe an invisible force will assist you? Thus, you may well begin to enjoy the life you deserve to live. You resisted the temptation, and you survived. It's almost as if *hope* never left your soul.

All-in-all the Jupiter-Saturn-Pluto conjunction is like a cheerful greeting for sobriety and darkness

ADDITIONAL INSPECTIONS

The Transformation of Romania

At the end of April 2027, we will most likely hear about certain events occurring in Romania. These happenings could represent the seeds for significant future events that will transpire later. Important clues to these events could *unfold* during March, April and May of 2028. Pluto transiting Romania's seventh house will reach eight degrees of Aquarius – a time when Pluto will be opposite natal Saturn (Leo in the 1st). Exactly what Pluto brings to the surface could be in total contradiction to the current strategy of Romania's government, their rules, and their principles. This could be the first, and a very serious measure, that might give the whole of Romania a difficult time.

Later, at the end of March 2033, Romania may experience another difficult period, which may transpire as a 'near death' experience. Thus, Pluto will conjunct Romania's Sun (see chart). Therefore, the overall identity of Romania may suffer to the point of new redefinition, political transformation, new reforms, and be given a new identity in the world.

Alternatively, on March 30, 2033, a solar eclipse at ten degrees of Aries falls directly in Romania's ninth house, and close to the MC. This could suggest that the countries' foreign affairs might by subjected to alteration – by changing its international relationships, treaties and alliances with other countries. This is a fire-cardinal eclipse, ruled by Mars – the planet of war and

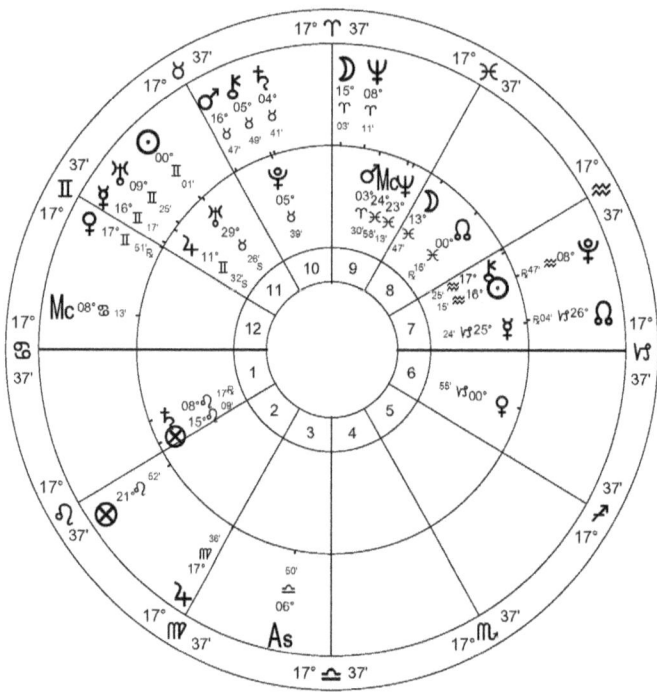

Chart 50: Inner wheel Romania natal: February 5, 1859, 14:41 LMT, Bucharest, Romania

Outer wheel: Transits May 20, 2028, 2:41 PM, Bucharest, Romania

competition. Romania's trading agreements with other countries may also be affected because of external hostilities. With an Aries MC, Romania has experienced hostilities from external aggressors many times throughout its history.

Moreover, Romania could look for support from its allies and communal organizations by asking for help, helping to heal the nation's wounds. Healing will be assisted with Chiron transiting Romania's eleventh house, which will restore the country's hopes and wishes, especially for the future of the nation. Furthermore, on April 14, 2033, a lunar eclipse at twenty-five degrees of Li-

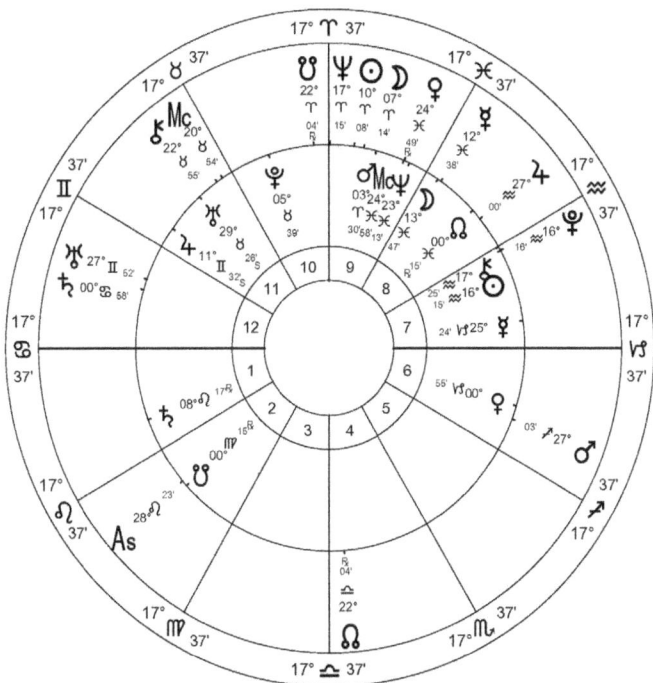

Chart 51: Inner wheel Romania natal: February 5, 1859, 14:41 LMT, Bucharest, Romania

Outer wheel: March 30, 2033, 2:41 PM, Bucharest, Romania

bra falls in Romania's fourth house. The eclipse will also square Romania's Mercury in the seventh house, possibly strengthening the nation's impartial foundations and creating new forms of diplomacy for the government. These transformational occurrences may well continue through to January 2035.

Pluto will transit Romania's Sun at sixteen degrees of Aquarius creating a combustion. For a time however, the country may not be able see its way forward. As Pluto begins to separate from the Sun beginning in January 2035 – *optimism* and *clear visibility* will slowly return to the government of Romania. This transfor-

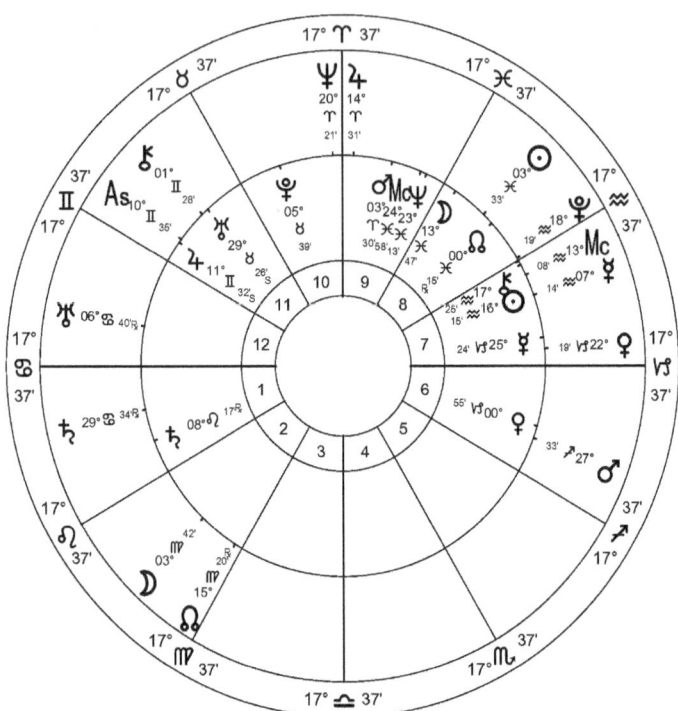

Chart 52: Inner wheel Romania natal: February 5, 1859, 14:41 LMT, Bucharest, Romania

Outer wheel: Lunar Eclpise February 22, 2035, 10:54 AM Bucharest, Romania

mation will be extended through February of 2035. The effects of this evolutionary transit will last approximately 248 years before Pluto returns to Romania's Sun.

The dawning of a new era could be *affirmed* by the February 2035 lunar eclipse at three degrees of Virgo. The lunar eclipse also conjuncts Romania's South Node at zero degrees of Virgo (an anaretic degree).[1] A lunar eclipse normally suggests a completion, and the South Node, a loss. However, the eclipse's opposition to the North Node in the eighth house (Pluto's natural house), implies a transformation of its values, and its national resources.

In addition, we could see a massive transformation of the nation's overall security. Thus, entirely new safeguards may be put into place as a result. Whatever the outcome, it is certain that Romania (my home country) is about to undertake an evolutionary transformation, unlike anything it has experienced in its recent history.

Chart Data:

Natal Chart for Romania, February 5, 1859, 14:41 LMT, Bucharest, Mean Node.

Reference

[1] Known as the anaretic (critical) degree, or the degree of fate. Anaretic degrees normally represent the end or the beginning of a cycle, hence twenty–nine, or zero degrees of a sign. A planet that falls on an anaretic degree is often restricted from expressing itself fully; similar to planets that are intercepted. Anaretic degrees are also associated with weakness and destruction.

Pluto and China

I thought it was important to conclude with an analysis of China, and its powerful influence on the rest of the world. There are several natal charts for China, but I think these are perhaps the most definitive of all:

On December 20, 2019, the Saturn-Pluto conjunction transited China's Jupiter, which lies at 22 degrees of Capricorn, in China's twelfth house. As a result, this configuration marks the beginning of a reticent, but powerful Saturn-Pluto expression, that may affect the entire world – emerging initially from China's twelfth house.

When Pluto transits over critical points, such as the Ascendant, the Descendant, the IC, and the MC, and especially over a natal planet of a country, it always rewrites the history of the nation concerned. However, China did *trigger* a global crisis – that began on the twelfth of January 2020 – an evolutionary juncture in which Saturn and Pluto made an exact conjunction.

Future Perspective

Looking further ahead, Pluto will begin its transit of Aquarius in April 2023. At this point, Pluto will conjunct China's Ascendant – marking a time of potential turbulence for this secretive republic state. Later, Pluto turns retrograde and moves back into Capricorn (Saturn's ruling sign). So, the already outdated rules and outspent power-play of this country will begin

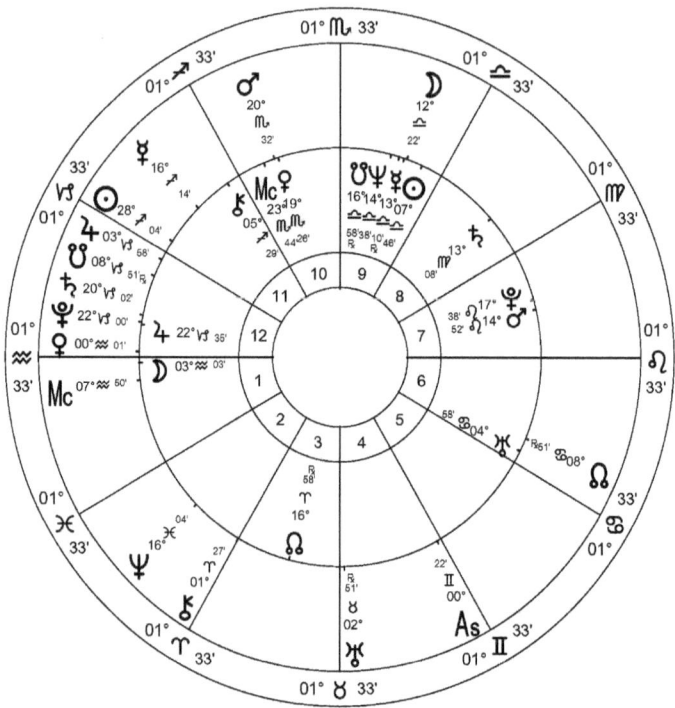

Chart 53: China natal: *October 1, 1949, 15:01 PM, Beijing, China*
Event Chart for China: *December 20, 2019, 3:01 PM, Beijing, China*

to emerge once more primarily because Pluto will transit China's Ascendant at the end of February 2024. I call this: 'a near death experience;' hence, a reconfiguration of government power, which will reconfigure a whole new identity for the country, and its citizens.

It might however orchestrate total change for China; and it may signify the end of the old communist regime? It may also increase interior and domestic power, but if we examine Pluto's trajectory through China's chart, we can see that Pluto will tran-

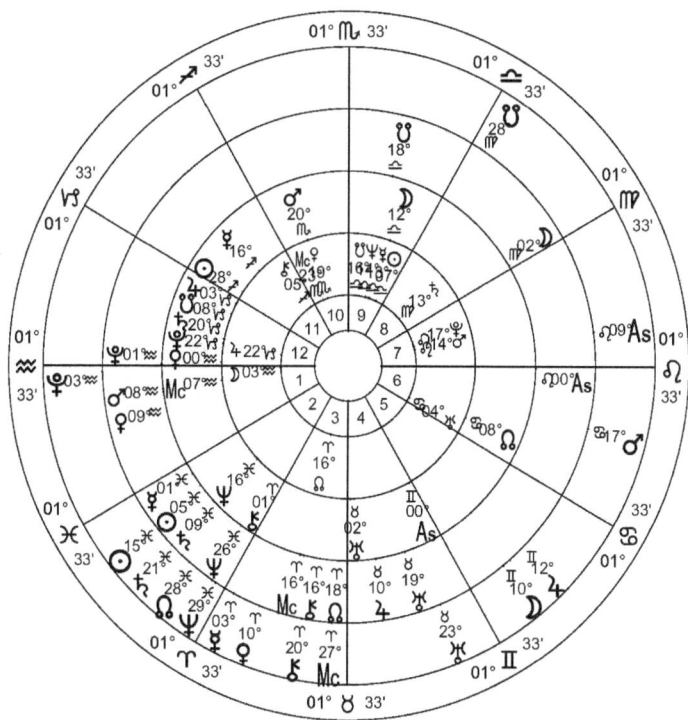

Chart 54: *Inner wheel China natal: October 1, 1949, 3:01 PM, Beijing, China*

Second wheel Event Chart for China, December 20, 2019, 3:01 PM, Beijing, China

Third wheel Event Chart China: February 24, 2024, 3:01 PM, Beijing, China

Outer wheel Event Chart China: March 6, 2025, 3:01 PM, Beijing, China

sit China's Moon at the beginning of March 2025. The Moon symbolizes the overall population of the country, while Pluto brings about what we already know. So, in a negative way, this transit of Pluto and the Moon could instill 'mass depression' throughout the entire population of China.

My Very Best Wishes

Maria Stiopei

Chart Data:

- Natal Chart for China, October 1, 1949, 15:01 PM, Beijing, China. Equal House system, Mean Node.
- Transit Chart for China, December 20, 2019, 15:01 PM, Beijing, China. Equal House system, Mean Node.
- Transit Chart for China, February 24, 2024, 15:01 PM, Beijing, China. Equal House system, Mean Node.
- Transit Chart for China, March 6, 2025, 15:01 PM, Beijing, China. Equal House system, Mean Node.

Charts Data:

Equal House Systems:

Chart 1.

Juan Garcia Ábrego, born: September 13, 1944, 2:00 AM, Matamoros, Mexico

Chart 2.

Angela Merkel, born: July 17, 1954, 6:00 PM, Hamburg, Germany

Chart 3.

Viktor Yanukovych, born: July 9, 1950, 12:15 PM, Jenakijevo, UA

Chart 4.

Lady Gaga, born: March 28, 1986, 9:53 AM, Manhattan, New York, USA

Chart 5.

Mueller Robert, born: August 7, 1944, New York, New York, USA (time unknown)

Chart 6.

Henry James, born: April 15, 1843, 2:00 PM, New York, New York, USA

Chart 7.

Larry King, born: November 19, 1933, 10:38 AM, Brooklyn, New York, USA

Chart 8.

Charles De Gaulle, born: November 22, 1890, 4:00 AM, Lille, FR

Chart 9.

Charles Harvey, born: June 22, 1940, 9:16 AM, Little Bookham, ENG (UK)

Chart 10.

Volodymyr Zelensky, born: January 25, 1978, 2:00 PM, Krivoj Rog, UA

Chart 11.

Mark Zuckerberg, born: May 14, 1984, White Plains, New York, (time unknown)

Chart12.

Joyce Carol Oates, born: June 16, 1938, 0:27 AM, Lockport, New York, USA

Chart 13.

Virginia Woolf, born: January 25, 1882, 12:15 PM, London, England

Chart 14.

Kim Jong Un, born: January 8, 1984, Pjongyang, Korea, North, (time unknown)

Chart 15.

Hugo Chavez, born: July 28, 1954, 4:00 AM, Sabaneta, Venezuela

Chart 16.

Ioan Clamparu, born: October 29, 1968, Botosani, Romania (time unknown)

Chart 17.

Warren Edward Buffett, born: August 30, 1930, 3:00PM,

Omaha, Nebraska, USA

Chart 18.

Bill Gates, born: October 28, 1955, 10:00 PM, Seattle, Washington, USA

Chart 19.

Serena Williams, born: Septemberr 26 19881, 8:28 PM, Saginaw, Michigan, USA

Chart 20.

Liz Greene, born: September 4, 1946, 1:01 PM, Englewood, New Jersey, USA

Chart 21.

Edward Snowden, born: June 21, 1983, 4:42 AM, Elizabeth City, North Carolina, USA

Chart 22.

Steven Spielberg, born: December 18, 1946, 6:16 PM, Cincinnati, OH, USA

Chart 23.

Sigmund Freud, born: May 6, 1856, 6:30 PM, Freiberg/Mahren, Czech Republic

Chart 24.

E.H. Troinski, born: December 18, 1910, 11:45 PM, Berlin, Germany

Chart 25.

Jeff Bezon, born: January 12, 1964, 12:00 PM, Albuquerque, New Mexico (time unknown)

Chart 26.

Bashar al Assad, born: September 11, 1965, Damascus, Syria (time unknown)

Chart 27

Momcilo Luburici, born: February 10, 1924, Bilec, Yugoslavia

Chart 28

Oprah Winfrey, born: January 29, 1954, 4:30 AM, Kosciusko, MS, USA

Chart 29

Quentin Tarantino, born: March 27 1963, 12:00 PM, Knoxville, TN

Chart 30

Lombroso Cesare, born: November 6, 1835, 11:00 PM, Verona , Italy

Chart 31

Eusapia Paladino, born: January 20, 1854, 7:00 PM, Minervino, Murge, Italy

Chart 32

E. E. Cummings, born: October 14, 1894, 7:00 PM, Cambridge, MA, USA

Chart 33

Vladimir Putin, born: October 7, 1952, 9:30 AM, St. Petersburg, Russia

Chart 34

William Frederick Allan, born: August 7, 1860, 5:49 AM, Westminster, England

Chart 35

Thomas Hardy, born: June 2, 1840, 8:00 AM, Dorset, England

Chart 36

Alphonse Bertillon, born: April 22, 1853, 9:00 AM, Paris France

Chart 37

Hermann Kummell, born: May 22, 1852, 6:30 PM, Korrbach, Germany

Chart 38

Emile Durkheim, born: April 15, 1858, 0:30 AM, Epinal, France

Chart 39

Maria Stiopei, born: June 5, 1978, 2:55 AM, Sighetul Marmatiei, Romania

Chart 40

USA Chart natal: July 4, 1776, 5:10 PM, Philadephia, PA (12°21" Sagittarius Ascendant)

Chart 41

Pluto transits 2000/21 over USA Chart (three wheels):

Inner Wheel: USA Natal Chart

Middle Wheel: January 31, 2000, 8;46 AM, New York

Outer Wheel: September 9, 2001, 8:46 AM, New York

Chart 42

Pluto transits 2014 over USA Chart (bi-wheels):

Inner wheel: USA natal chart

Outer Wheel: February 2, 2014, 2:49 New York

Chart 43

Pluto transits 2021/27 over USA Chart (three wheels):

Inner Wheel: USA natal chart

Middle Wheel: April 23, 2021, 5:10 PM, New York

Outer Wheel: April 16, 2027, 8:46 AM, New York

Chart 44

United Kingdom natal: December 25, 1066, 12:00 PM,

Westminster, England

Chart 45

Pluto transits 2016/19 over UK Chart (three wheels):
Inner Wheel: UK natal chart
Middle Wheel: June 23, 2016, 12:00 PM, London, UK
Outer Wheel: March 29, 2019, 11:00 PM, London, UK

Chart 46

Pluto transits 2023/2024 over UK Chart (three wheels):
Inner Wheel: UK natal chart
Middle Wheel: March 16, 2023, 12:00 PM, London, UK
Outer Wheel: September 11, 2024, 12:00 PM, London, UK

Chart 47

Pluto transits 2028 over UK Chart (bi-wheels):
Inner Wheel: UK natal chart
Outer Wheel: March 30, 2028, 12:00 PM, London, UK

Chart 48

NATO: April 4, 1949, 4:45 PM, Washington D.C.

Chart 49

Pluto transits 1969/2023 over NATO chart (tri-wheel):
Inner wheel: NATO: April 4, 1949, 4:45 PM, Washington D.C.
Middle Wheel: August 11, 1969, 4:45 PM
Outer Wheel: February 12, 2023, 4:45 PM

Chart 50

Romania Bi-wheel, Inner wheel: Romania natal: February 5, 1859, 2:41 PM, Bucharest, Romania

Outer wheel: Transits May 20, 2028, EET -2:00, Bucharest, Romania

Chart 51

Romania Bi-wheel, Inner wheel: Romania natal: February 5, 1859, 2:41 PM, EET -2:00, Bucharest, Romania

Outer wheel: Transits March 30, 2033, 2:41 PM EET -2:00, Bucharest, Romania

Chart 52

Romania Bi-wheel, Inner wheel: Romania natal: February 5, 1859, 2:41 PM, Bucharest, Romania

Outer wheel: Lunar Eclipse February 22, 2035, EET - 2:00, Bucharest, Romania

Chart 53

China Bi-wheel, Inner wheel: China natal: October 1, 1949, 3:01 PM, Beijing, China

Outer wheel: Transit Event December 20, 2019, 3:01 PM, Beijing, China

Chart 54

China Quad-wheel:

Inner wheel: China natal: October 1, 1949, 3:01 PM, Beijing, China

Second wheel: Transit Event December 20, 2019, 3:01 PM, Beijing, China

Third Wheel: Transit Event February 24, 2024, 3:01 PM, Beijing, China

Outer wheel: Transit Event March 6, 2025, 3:01 PM, Beijng, China

www.ingramcontent.com/pod-product-compliance
Lightning Source LLC
Chambersburg PA
CBHW051127160426
43195CB00014B/2377